AFRICAN ART

PIERRE MEAUZÉ

Curator of the Musée
des Arts Africains et Océaniens in Paris

AFRICAN ART

Sculpture

THE WORLD PUBLISHING COMPANY

Cleveland and New York

The author and publishers wish to thank all those who,
through their publications and their knowledge,
have contributed to the preparation of this book.
They also wish to thank the directors of museums and the private collectors
who have given permission for works of art, often little known,
in their collections to be photographed and reproduced, and have thus
contributed to a better understanding of African art.

Note : A glossary explaining the words followed by an asterisk will be found at the end of the book.

Published by The World Publishing Company
2231 West 110th Street, Cleveland, Ohio 44102

Published simultaneously in Canada by
Nelson, Foster & Scott Ltd.

First Edition

© 1968 by Meulenhoff International, Amsterdam

Photographs © 1967 by André Held, Lausanne

English translation © 1968 by Weidenfeld and Nicolson Ltd., London

Library of Congress Catalog Card Number : 67 $\frac{I}{N}$ 24467

Printed in Switzerland by Held S. A., Lausanne

CONTENTS

INTRODUCTION

Before we can experience the impact and beauty of African art, do we have to forsake the Western culture which we have inherited and which conditions the way our very eyes perceive ? Do we have to undergo an aesthetic brainwash ?

It is clearly no longer necessary to ask this question now that Africa has begun to be integrated with the West and the rest of the world. Such a question, moreover, slights the culture we are about to discover. We would not dream of asking a Senegalese, an Ivory Coast or a Cameroon Negro to renounce his culture in order to study our Western art and react to it as we do, if only for a moment. Only a proper exchange of views about our respective cultures, starting from well-defined aesthetic and scientific bases, will enable us to appraise the aesthetic values of Africa, and will enable the Africans to analyse the somewhat confused creative problems of the Western world. For, even if — with the help of Islam — we have been to some extent the assassins of African art, is it not true that various European phenomena, including the constant increase of visual knowledge, have greatly confused even our greatest artists, often inducing them to depart from their true roots ? The result is that large areas of our contemporary art are going adrift.

If art is to continue to exist, some such new exchange of knowledge will help to establish a kind of universal plastic language. Perhaps such a development is not desirable, but it is very likely inevitable.

PURPOSE OF THE BOOK

This book does not aim at defining African art in its overall expression; it merely tries to cast light — to a great extent thanks to the exceptional clearness and sharpness of the photography — on the large masks and statues inspired by everyday occurrences, and to view them with the somewhat fearful and respectful detachment, appropriate to objects imbued with magic. Some of the masterpieces attain the almost unbearable intensity and impenetrability that are elsewhere found only in some Egyptian sculptures of the Golden Age. The vigour of the large African masks is expressed without restraint and asserts itself heedless of any sensibility it may upset. But it is the sculptor's hand which shapes this power.

AFRICAN ART AND EUROPE

At the beginning of this century the great artists reacted to the revelation of African sculpture as to the advent of a ' Black Messiah '.

Like religion, art has its miracles, and it was a miracle for Picasso, Braque, Derain, Vlaminck and Matisse to find an answer to their misgivings and, if not guidance, at least a means of breaking loose from conventional forms and re-exploring the field of plastic invention, thus opening the door — at last — to total freedom.

Thus, we should be speaking of a convergence rather than of an influence. The inventors of Cubism and of Fauvism were seduced by the visible forms of African sculpture. They did not try — and had they tried they would not have succeeded — to understand the meaning of these sculptures and the deep ties which linked them to the culture from which they arose. Eventually, Fernand Léger made use of the Ivory Coast masks for the setting and costumes of the Negro ballet *The Creation of the World*. This, however, was nothing more than an accurate reference.

Only more recently have Max Ernst (in a number of sculptures), Brancusi and Gonzalez achieved an almost complete synthesis through which certain African plastic principles acquire universal symbolic value.

We make no claim to have produced an exhaustive or scientific work; none the less, we would never have been able to find our way amidst this ethnic variety and, eventually, to compare the various styles and set the masterpieces in their proper light without the important and increasingly accurate discoveries of our best research workers.

The wide knowledge of such scholars as Marcel Griaule, Michel Leiris, Denise Paulme, Jacqueline Delange, William and Bernard Fagg, A. Maesen, Elsy Leuzinger, Robert Goldwater and Margaret Plass have contributed and are still contributing greatly to a synthesis based on observation and definition. These art-loving ethnologists have always approached African art with a sort of questioning respect, prepared to encounter the unexpected which compels admiration and even passion and is an introduction to the mystery of knowledge.

To analyse this ' knowledge-love ' phenomenon is outside our scope, but it remains a fact

BIDJOGO. Helmet-mask in basket-work covered with leather and inlaid with red ' abrus precatorius ' seeds and cowrie shells — which were for a long time used as money in Africa. This mask has real horns and represents the bull, symbol of virility. Specimens of the same type, but much larger and entirely in wood, decorated the bows of war canoes as recently as half a century ago.

8   *Height: 68 cm.   Bidjogo (Bissago Islands - Portuguese Guinea).   Angoulême Municipal Museum.*

which accounts for most of the work ever to have been undertaken in human studies. However, if approached by minds lacking in warmth and 'attentiveness' (in Gide's sense of the word), all this labour would remain arid and schematic.

Today, thanks to increasingly complete publications and exhibitions, a much greater if not complete revelation is available to the artist, who no longer merely studies forms and relationships but tries to get to the very essence of artistic creation, to its links with the real life of mankind. This may even lead to a new awareness — large-scale cross-breedings have often proved beneficial.

It is still too early for African art to be re-evaluated by the Africans themselves: those who might attempt to do so are in effect cut off from their original background (with the exception of people like Hampate Ba, Sheik Anta Diop and a few others who, to paraphrase Cocteau, 'sing in their genealogical tree'). Were the arts of the Middle Ages and the art of Egypt really understood before the nineteenth century ? We shall have to wait for the various trends in the analysis of art to converge — which incidentally is under way — in order to arrive at a synthesis to which the Africans, prompted by faith and method and acquiring consciousness of their past cultural values, will contribute new concepts arising from original creative centres. This, however, will not be achieved in the near future, for many gaps must be filled before such a stage is reached. It will require more archaeological research supplemented by

BAGA. Drum. The hieratic attitude of the kneeling woman presenting her child calls to mind the twelfth century Catalan Madonnas. The drum is supported by small caryatids. A similar example, probably by the same sculptor, is now at the British Museum; its upper part is removable.
Hardwood with natural patina. Height: 111 cm. Baga (Coastal Guinea). Maurice Nicaud Collection, Paris.

II

precise definition and dating and a more thorough study of the extremely rich but still not properly defined material.

Therefore, all that we can do now, is to look deeper into this particular form of art, allow ourselves to become permeated with it and react to its undiminished power and vigour. The art of sculpture, this fundamental form of expression, retains all its power and nobility whatever its size, and under *cowrie-shells**, crusted blood, fabrics and bells, mirrors and shells, the form stands out or may be guessed in all its nakedness and inherent power. The truth of African art lies in this fundamental power, and if men were more curious, more clear-minded and more honest, this power would explode before their very eyes.

STATUS OF THE AFRICAN ARTIST

Hampate Ba, one of the most profound philosophers of Mali and heir to important traditions, tells us that, in all the countries of the Sudan, 'weavers, sculptors, potters and smiths were members of exclusive societies in which the masters, assisted by their servants, taught the apprentices the sacred craft. Rather than derive money therefrom, they devoted themselves to this sacred craft in order to please the gods and the spirits of ancestors'.

This circumstance turned craftsmen into special men, classed according to their crafts. They were dreaded masters, capable of neutralising or unleashing at will the forces of nature either to punish or to reward.

While this is true of the Sudanese grasslands, it does not necessarily apply to the coastal countries, the inhabitants of lagoon areas and the Ashanti, Dahomey and Congolese chiefdoms where craftsmen and workshops, though enjoying relative freedom, were handicapped in their creative activity by the power of society at all levels. The Negro artist has long been falsely understood; stereotyped notions have subordinated African sculpture to a social and religious system capable of no more than reproducing images, masks and statues, which were always alike, and which acquired value only after having been consecrated and blessed by the high-ranking members of secret societies in ritual ceremonies.

Therefore, the idea of a creator, alive with emotions, capable of concentration, of studying shapes and pondering them, of comprehensive composition as well as refinement of detail, never occurred to scholars approaching Negro art for the first time. In recent years, however, no ethnologist of importance has failed to discover 'his' sculptor or sculptors, sometimes even their names and villages. Now with a wider field of investigation, comparative studies often enable us to identify with accuracy the works of a given master of wood or bronze.

BAGA. Represents Kakilembe, supreme god of the Baga. A sort of synthesis of bird, fish and man. Kept in a secret place, it is taken out every seven years during public ceremonies.
Painted, very hard wood. Height: 141 cm. Baga (Coastal Guinea). Maurice Nicaud Collection, Paris.

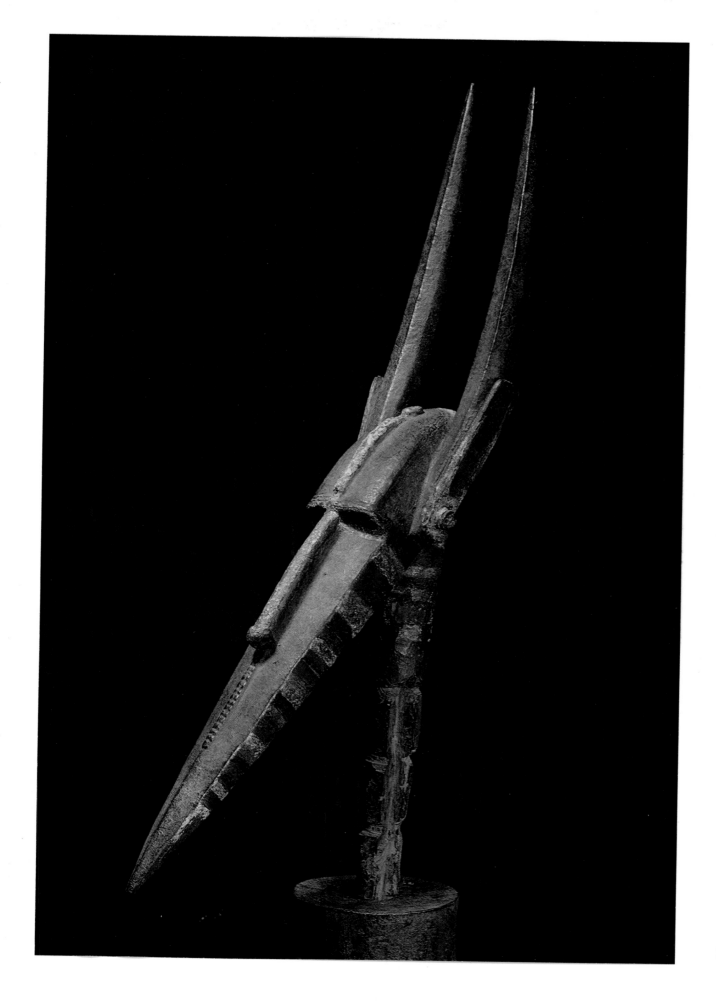

When the Abidjan Museum was set up over twenty-five years ago, it became easier to find *in situ* Baule or Guro sculptors whose very personal creations (smiling mask, page 73), though conforming to an accepted and traditional style, bore a real stamp, an actual signature as it were. We may even go a step further and discover that the Negro artist is literally possessed by an uncanny genius, as if form — conscious only of its organic development and natural splendour — had shaken itself free from the creative hand and the accidents of technique and human effort to become sheer essence. We refer in particular to the *Chi wara* antelope (page 148 top) in the Nicaud Collection: here is a masterpiece which does not go against the current, but is the unexpected tributary of its own style. This proves that Africa has its individual artists who are aware of the value and power of their creation, just like the twelfth-century stone cutters whom we have been led to think of as anonymous and obscure. Not to understand that sculpture is one of the most intense, most difficult, most profound, most introspective and therefore personal of all human activities is to ignore the meaning of carving, this long dialogue between man and matter — be it stone or wood.

POWER OR CHARM

Though it is impossible to get to the essence of these various forms, a panoramic glance is sufficient to encompass most if not all of them. Our eclectic sensibility is attracted from the start towards such reassuring styles as those of Ife, Baule and Baluba art. Every time we contemplate a magnificent Ife bronze mask (page 179), we realise that it will always retain its rightful place, immovable in its detached serenity. But does it tell us anything of Africa during the century when it was created?

When classical art was at its height, striving for the perfection of forms often damped the deep internal impulse. We must look for Africa elsewhere, in statues humbler in appearance, more rudimentary, of more spontaneous inspiration. We must investigate the rigid and cold ancestral statues of the Oron, remotely reminiscent of a Chartres portal, the Yoruba ivory statuettes with their compact and austere shapes which emanate power.

May we dare a rather romantic speculation? Why not assume that, when completing his work, the artist (painter or sculptor) encloses a physical force in the mask or statue, locks it up as it were, and that this force is eventually restored to us by some kind of radiation process which we may learn to measure? This would call for a sort of talent- or genius-measuring Geiger counter. Whatever the case may be, there is no doubt that certain masterpieces which only

SHERBRO. Stone carved in the shape of a figure in a recumbent position with legs crossed. This type of sculpture, called 'nomoli', undoubtedly represents ancestors and was formerly used during funeral rituals. The 'nomoli' are now considered beneficent powers which fecundate the earth and favour the cultivation of rice. Soft soapstone. Length: 36 cm.   Sherbro (Sierra Leone Republic).   British Museum, London.

15

subjective emotion is able to define as such, literally 'emanate' waves of attraction, and though they do not necessarily arouse admiration, they always exercise a spell.

THE VEILED GODS

History shows that the importance of the word 'worship' has considerably diminished throughout the centuries, even in the heart of Africa. Taking as an example the mythical Dogon — the eight fundamental wise men — we cannot fail to see that they are featured less and less; we do know of the existence of, among others, Kakilembe, supreme god of the Baga (page 13), and the large Bobo-Fing mask (page 45). Is Islam, here as elsewhere, responsible for this fear of display, or is it a trend of a society evolving towards secular values where chiefs have taken and are taking more and more the place of gods, replacing the divine features with their own image and, though not wiping out the gods altogether, throwing them into shade? Probably it was this trend that gave origin to the Ghana, Dahomey, Benin, Cameroon and Bakuba 'court art'. Like Western Christianity, increasingly showy and pompous but moving further and further away from the embarrassing asceticism of Christ, the feudal organisation of royal courts and great chiefdoms cast aside and dimmed whatever was too exacting and present in these gods.

VARIETY AND QUALITY

The large number of African sculptures we are now able to see in Western museums and collections is only a part of what Africa has produced: no final conclusions can be drawn from these works; by numerous comparisons we can arrive at no more than tentative observations. Let us imagine a really well-qualified scholar, someone like Henri Focillon, coming across specimens of French Romanesque art removed from their architectural setting: works of the twelfth to fourteenth centuries, in wood, stone, ivory, metal, copper or gold. How many of them would stand out from the mass of hasty images and commonplace repetitions? Style bears its masterpieces as the sea bears its ships: congestion is rare. Luckily those less favoured benefit from the beauty and radiance of these masterpieces — this makes for power in style.

ART AND MAN

Probably no other art objects have ever been so carefully handled and fondled as have many of the objects, statuettes and masks of Negro Africa.

SENUFO. Dance mask from a Senufo sub-tribe, east of Korhogo. Hardwood with lacquered patina. The stylised form of a bird, reduced to little more than its beak, is added to the forehead of the mask. Nevertheless, this mask has on its cheeks the two small ritual 'legs' which are supposed to link it to the earth.
Black wood. Height: 35 cm.   Senufo (north-west of the Ivory Coast).   Clamagirand Collection, Paris.

16

The eye teaches the body to see and vice versa: a given type of sculpture is like an idea that can be touched, that can be looked at from all sides without ever exhausting its suggestiveness. The spiritual and even emotional links which bound the Africans to their protective symbols and their religious functions were intense and permanent. The warm and sensitive touch — for the hand transfers power and one learns to believe through touch — played a daily, essential role. This may account for the wonderful patina and transparency of the Warega masks, the Baluba statuettes and the small Bakongo reliquaries.

DANCE AND ITS SIGNIFICANCE

We must never forget that the art of the mask is intimately related to the dance. This extremely sensitive art is a dynamic expression which is turned to ice by museums and exhibitions. Is it too daring to imagine museums of the future in which new patterns and principles would supersede those we have inherited and which, despite innovations, still hamper us ?

Unlike Greek or Roman art, African art has no temples and awe-inspiring magic corridors where the solitary human being feels himself plunged into a universe which subdues and cripples him. Here the human being comes into contact with vital forces, elements and forms which, transfigured, are life itself gushing out from every source. Here the senses are stirred, nurtured and elated, and the true destiny of art is revealed: to transplant man, to carry him elsewhere.

ULTIMATE DESTINY

The Egyptian pyramids — tokens of survival, challenge to death, ultimate shelter — and the Gothic cathedrals — everlasting songs, as permanent as a theme by Bach to which it seems there should be no end — defy our notions of time. African art is light, almost always roving and portable; no sooner born, it is fated to disappear, a fact recognised and accepted by both maker and user.

What we, Africans and Westerners alike, are trying to do now — to produce exhibitions, museums, confrontations, studies and research — may seem contrary to the original destiny of Negro art. Are we to give up these pursuits, now that the world, increasingly aware of and attracted by its art-producing minorities, is being enriched by beauty, wisdom and history which it previously ignored and might never have known ?

SENUFO. Double mask in light bronze. The origin of these masks has often been contested: in fact, a quite prosperous craftsmanship still produces them daily. However, this and a few other examples known to us — as well as a certain number of bronzes, cups and chief's insignia similar to the Dahomey recados — seem to us authentically traditional, as testified by the imposing archaism of the face.
Height: 26 cm.   Senufo-Korhogo (north-west of the Ivory Coast).   Henri Kamer Collection, Cannes.

HISTORICAL SURVEY

PRELIMINARY INQUIRY

To date, apart from the relatively imprecise material provided by the Tassili frescoes, we know of no African archaeology earlier than the fifth century BC. The Greeks were familiar only with what is now called Libya. However, Herodotus had already referred to 'men with hair more curly than that of others', who were probably Negroes. Therefore we have reason to believe that the Nubians were of negroid origin and that Negro Africa, with which we are here concerned, once extended further to the north than it has in recent times. If we accepted the existence of a Nubian civilisation earlier than that of pre-dynastic Egypt and its expansion to the south as well as to the north, we could conclude that the ancient Negro races have given an ideological and plastic contribution to Mediterranean civilisations. This, however, is merely an exciting hypothesis; we hope that science will establish with certainty the facts amidst this mixture of passions, racial anxieties, claims to civilisation and alleged 'cultural superiorities'.

EVIDENCE OF THE FRESCOES

Among the documentary evidence relating to some two thousand frescoes and engravings on rock brought back by Henri Lhote from his various expeditions to Tassili, we find many references to masks worn by dancers. (The body of the man wearing the mask can easily be made out.) In a specific instance — a tracing made at Inawanrhet in 1957 — the style of the mask is not dissimilar to the Senufo style, while other elements of the same mask are reminiscent of the Cameroon style; this, however, is merely a tentative analysis. According to Carbon-fourteen tests this fresco can be dated to around 5000 BC. We know that Carbon-fourteen is an isotope contained in organic bodies and that its radioactivity weakens with time, thus making it possible to date the work, though with no great accuracy. However, in such a case it is of great importance to be able to go so far back in time even with a margin for error of up to a thousand years. This seven-thousand-year-old mask traced at Inawanrhet is evidence of a tradition maintained despite upheavals, the transformation of forests into deserts, mass migrations, clashes between peoples. The ritual significance of the first mask may well have been different from that of more recent ones, the real meaning of which we are only beginning to discover. It would not

SENUFO. Large statue in patinated and coloured wood. Brown background, white and red decorations. Human figure surmounted by a hollowed-out disc, the ritual hair-dress of candidates for the society of ironsmiths. Used during induction ceremonies of this brotherhood, to appeal for the protection and aid of ancestors. Height: 115 cm.   Senufo (north-west of the Ivory Coast).   Museum of Primitive Art, New York.

20

be the first time that an old shape is called to a new destiny: thus, in another field, the hermit-crab dwells in the shell of a dead mollusc.

PRESUMED LINKS

We are inclined to share Theodore Monod's opinion that the famous Ibibio statue (Nigeria) — a sort of goddess with snakes — 'irresistibly conjures up Aegean art'. At present there is a tendency to compare the large Axum *stelae* with the so-called 'multi-tiered' Dogon masks still used today. Dogon art offers other mysterious resemblances such as that of the seated couples; the well-known example owned by the Barnes Foundation and another, recently acquired by the Vincennes museum, are similar to the sculptured Pharaonic couples.

Moving towards the coast we find more relics which raise similar problems: some of the Senufo *Deble* (page 23) have the same triangular hair-dress as the Fourth Dynasty faces, while others (page 21) carry on their heads a solar disc in the shape of a crocodile, symbol of duration if not of eternity.

The disc-shaped faces of the *Akua ba* dolls and the engraved fans of the Ashanti call to mind the bronze mirrors in which the omnipresent golden sun is evoked, hence invoked.

Culture feeds on comparisons. Even if not always supported by scientific evidence, a certain freedom of the mind and the eye may lead us ultimately to new visions and new concepts.

ANCIENT NUBIA

Nubia (since 3000 BC) has been inhabited by a people who, though retaining a neolithic civilisation, have lost the characteristics of pre-dynastic Egypt to become a negroid race. In early times, Nubia was an important centre of trade with the southern regions, the Negro Africa of today. The Egyptians came regularly to Nubia to enroll Negro mercenaries, but there is nothing to prove that these were slaves. One thing is certain: Nubia was for a great many years the two-way channel connecting Northern Africa — Egypt and Libya — with the Negro peoples and their empires. Recent excavations have brought to light a type of very broad-faced Negro. Objects found at the same time — fragments of bones, pottery decorated with curves — seem to belong to the pre-dynastic period. Stone rings used for archery and iron arrow-heads suggest that the first people to inhabit the Upper Nile were hunters and fishermen of a negroid type.

The problem raised at the beginning of this book is to determine which of the White or Negro

SENUFO. Large wooden statue called 'Deble'. Used during initiation ceremonies: the lower part of the legs, the support and one of the woman's breasts are missing. The triangular hair-dress evokes Egyptian art.
Height: 102 cm.   Senufo (Ivory Coast).   Musée des Arts Africains et Océaniens, Paris.

African peoples originated the Egyptian dynastic civilisation and, by inference, the Greek and Roman civilisations as well. Or rather, more modestly, to try to assess the contribution of both races: the mythical beliefs, the basic cosmogonies, the plastic forms through which such systems of conceiving the world were translated into art.

Let us list a few illuminating facts :

— Numerous Egyptian bas-reliefs represent wild animals from Negro Africa. These animals have never dwelt on the banks of the Middle and Lower Nile; at least no trace of them has ever been found.

— In the Unas pyramid reference is made to violent tornadoes and steady rainfall: this corresponds in every detail to the description of tropical phenomena peculiar to the coastal forests of western and central equatorial Africa.

— In royal protocol the title of the king of the South, who was a Negro, ranked higher than that of the king of the North.

— Some of the Egyptian gods, like Amon and Osiris, were represented with black bodies; as for Isis, she was considered a black goddess. (Is it necessary to add that some contemporary Egyptians have clearly negroid features ?)

— Min, the phallic god, had a priest-servant called 'the Black'. The phallus, often associated with snake worship, is featured throughout Negro Africa.

As Assirelli writes in *Polyglot Africa*: 'The study of Africa is, as it were, an extension of Egyptology. '

Like the African gods, the gods of Egypt had in remote times been human beings, creators of cities and progenerators of primeval races rather than 'ideological gods', disembodied and remote. Maybe one of the few but also major shortcomings of Christianity is this lack of a physical creative source to which every human being responds and which even the highest spirituality cannot altogether replace.

THE SAO EMPIRE

The Kotoko, present inhabitants of what is supposed to have been the ancient Sao empire, consider themselves the descendants of these legendary people. The Arab manuscripts of Bornu refer to the past existence of giants called So. Today Sao is still the name of a village.

The names of Jean-Paul Lebeuf and Annie Masson-Detourbet are linked with the most important archaeological discoveries in Negro Africa as that of Bernard Fagg is associated

BAMBARA. Pair of antelopes called ' chi wara', carved in finely open-worked and decorated wood. They represent the male principle, on the one hand, and the female and maternal principles, on the other. These sculptures are fitted onto small baskets and worn during agricultural propitiatory dances.
Height: 90 cm.   Bambara (western region of the Mali Republic).   Clamagirand Collection, Paris.

24

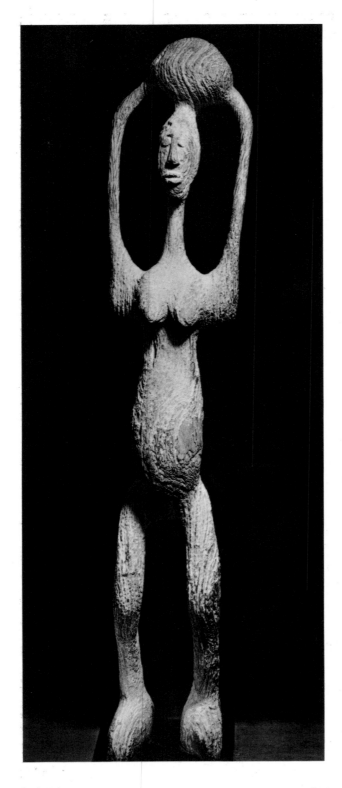

with the terracottas of the Nok civilisation.

The quantity and quality of material brought to light is remarkable and constitutes an inexhaustible field for further research.

New excavations near Fort-Lamy led to the discovery of the Tago sanctuary with its numerous ancient terracotta statuettes. These are anthropomorphous figures, sometimes with animal heads — bulls, hippopotami and rams; this is another feature also characteristic of Mediterranean civilisations. The 'human' faces of these statuettes are fashioned with such vehemence — bulging eyes, 'terraced' mouth, bridge of nose protruding like a horn — that one wonders whether any real reference to man was intended. The plastic creations of the Sao seem to represent a departure from the usual African context, for all its variety (and the African continent offers to the world a vast range of new forms). However, despite this dizzying inventiveness, the enigmatic logic of forms remains; despite the disturbing outward appearance and the emotion caused by the first impact, these works attain final structural stability and poise.

We might regard Sao art as monstrous in the strict meaning of the word. Is this frenzied modelling which still suggests the presence of the sculptor's hand the work of diabolical, inhibited creatures who deliberately banished all reference to reality in order to instil this terrific power ? It is more reassuring to seek in these faces—of which some look like men turned into toads and others with human features — a fusion between the powers of Water and Earth, a sort of rediscovered mythical relationship. Once again, this dual aspect brings us to the well-

BAMBARA. Large sculpture in natural hardwood, very much eroded by time. Probably the evocation of an ancestor. The attitude of the bearer, simplified to the extreme, goes beyond the anecdotal and becomes a symbol. Height: 135 cm. Bambara (western region of the Mali Republic). Henri Kamer Collection, Cannes.

26

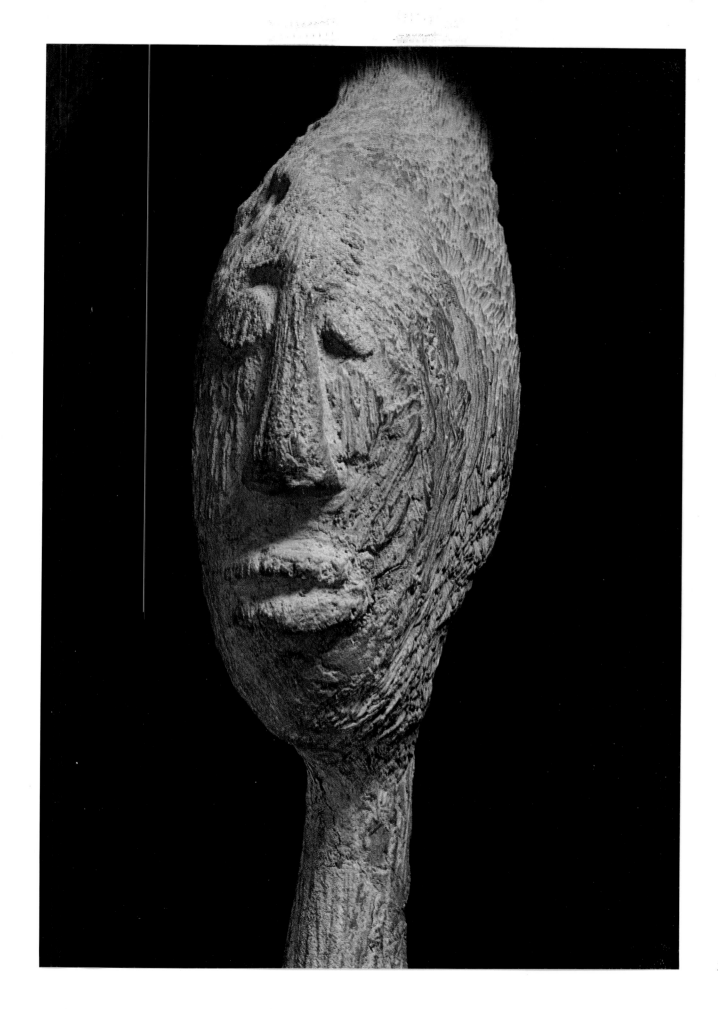

known Egyptian pantheon of animal-gods.

In order to 'locate' the documents essential for an understanding of the Sao, Kotoko and Fali, we must again refer to J.-P. Lebeuf. First of all there are already-quoted Arab manuscripts; then there is a text by Makrisi, a fourteenth-century geographer who referred to the Kotoko country; later, in 1906, Asselin and Houzeau confirmed the alleged descent of the Kotoko from a race of giants. Their empire is believed to have collapsed by the end of the fifteenth century when they were defeated by the sultan Edriss Alaoma. The cruel henna episode related by de Pedrals refers to that period: 'Seeing the Arabs dye their nails with henna, the So asked to be taught how to do it. Taking advantage of the moment when the hands of the artless So were imprisoned in vessels filled with henna, the Arabs put them to the sword.' There are two Kotoko versions of this episode, both referring to the Sao as black giants having come from remote countries beyond the desert. The presence of huge stones at the gates of Gulfei seems to corroborate this tradition which, after all, may not be altogether legendary. In any case, the Kotoko, probable descendents of the Sao, consider stone sacred; they use stone altars in all important ceremonies. Incidentally, during a Roman Catholic mass, the 'sacrifice' must be celebrated on a stone.

Let us mention further that the myth of the snake Makari is in every respect similar to the Egyptian tradition of the separation and dispersal of the limbs of Osiris. This myth tells of the attack and subsequent death of a fabulous snake which was beheaded by the victors and cut into seven

BAMBARA. Large wooden statue representing a seated woman supporting her breasts. Helmet-shaped hairstyle. This sculpture, probably featuring a queen, is undoubtedly linked with a fertility and fecundity cult. Height: 102 cm. Bambara (Buguni-Doïla region - Mali Republic). Museum of Primitive Art, New York.

28

pieces; the seven pieces were buried in seven different places, each of which became the centre of one of the seven districts of the city, while the Royal Palace was built on the spot where the head had been set down.

At the present stage of archaeology, many disconcerting data are both landmarks and question marks; here again we can only hope for future enlightenment.

Without coming to any definitive conclusions, we can accept that there once existed a race of men well exceeding two metres in height and coming in all likelihood from Ethiopia, and that the ancient civilisation of this astonishing race gradually declined and was ultimately annihilated, perhaps as a result of cross-breeding and, eventually, absorption.

MYSTERIOUS ZIMBABWE

In the sixteenth century, a Portuguese navigator named Goes was the first to report the existence, in the heart of Rhodesia, of a famous and mysterious stronghold built of stone without mortar. This site, known locally by the name of Symbave or Zimbabwe, still exists and consists of three adjacent but distinct constructions: the Great Temple, the Tower and the 'Acropolis', the latter erected on a hill and towering above the surrounding area.

Posselt visited Zimbabwe in 1888: 'When the porters came in sight of the monuments, they greeted them by clapping their hands and said that these were ruins of buildings in which the Barozwe offered sacrifices to their gods; when the explorer made an attempt to remove some of the carved birds decorating the outside of the walls, they assumed a threatening attitude.' The first excavations, headed by Hall, took place in 1904. Inside the wall surrounding the Great Temple, under a thin layer of hardened earth, was a sort of cement called *daga*; as soon as it was removed, the excavators started making discoveries: phallic-shaped steatite stones, cups decorated with animals or chevrons, pipes, beads of various origins, golden jewels, bracelets (for wrist or ankle), arrow-heads, a signal gong. The most astonishing discoveries were fragments of Chinese porcelain.

In 1929, Miss Caton-Thompson's systematic research led to important discoveries mainly concerning the interiors of dwellings, while further digging brought to light spiral-shaped fragments of bronze, potsherds and golden beads. Among the finds at the 'Acropolis' were multicoloured beads of definitely foreign origin, probably from the first century AD, fragments of glazed pottery and even of celadon, the latter undoubtedly Chinese.

Therefore we can assume that trade was very probable between this centre (was it a part of the *Monomotapa** kingdom?) and both India and China. Lack of historical data does not

DOGON. Female ancestor figure carrying a child. Hardwood covered with thick red deposit. The litheness of form of this masterpiece, which seems fairly old, does not impair its architectural stateliness. Height: 75 cm.   Dogon (northern region, Mali Republic).   Maurice Nicaud Collection, Paris.

31

allow us either to confirm or invalidate this assumption — only these strange relics are there to bear witness. The presence at Zimbabwe of golden objects and jewels does not mean that there were necessarily gold mines in this area if we accept the likelihood of commercial exchange being already in existence: in spite of its specific weight, gold is the lightest and most easily transportable currency.

One of the greatest difficulties the explorers had to face was the complete lack of any oral tradition. The races now inhabiting the area in which the ruins were discovered are silent on this subject. Basing herself on the study of beads, Miss Caton-Thompson dates life in Zimbabwe to the eighteenth and nineteenth centuries; this, however, seems to be a frail assumption. We have already referred to the steatite birds which, we know, decorated the walls of the Great Temple. A few of them are at the British Museum; one was at the Dahlem Museum, Berlin, but was destroyed, and others are to be found in the Rhodesian museums. Another hybrid and mysterious object causing uneasiness rather than emotion is the 'bird-man' of the Tishman collection, recently on display at the Musée de l'Homme, Paris. Only the carapace with wings folded back and possibly the base might justify its appellation, for otherwise it is of human appearance, with arms flat against the body and holes in the place of eyes (probably once filled with beads). One thing is certain: it is cut in a hard stone, quite different from the soapstone commonly used in this centre as well as in many other centres in Africa.

DOGON. Ancestral figure on horseback, of a mythical nature. Eroded natural wood with scarification on stomach and back. The compactness and simplicity of forms can be ascribed to the Dogon High Middle Ages. Remarkable for its powerful execution, its perfect state of preservation and its size.

32   *Height: 82 cm.*   *Dogon (northern region, Mali Republic).*   *Henri Kamer Collection, Cannes.*

Is Zimbabwe linked with a wider Rhodesian civilisation and, together with the Baluba and Barotse, to be regarded as part of the Monomotapa kingdom, or is it an island, an isolated and maybe unique phenomenon ?

IFE TRADITIONS

Ife may be considered the cradle of the very large Yoruba ethnic group which, we know, extended west through Dahomey and Togo, as far as present-day Ghana. In spite of great differences in religious ceremonies, a certain cultural unity prevails. All kings of the Yoruba kingdoms, including the Oni of Ife, the Oba of Benin and a few others — whether converted to Christianity or not — have a common link: they are depositaries of a sacred tradition.

Although present-day Ife is merely a historical capital with no great political importance, it retains, thanks to its glorious past, an evocative power. It is still considered by the large Yoruba population (several million inhabitants) as a holy city, a place of worship where gods were revealed to men for the first time. Once a capital, centre of the greatest secular and social power, it became, and probably will remain, a 'mythical' and mystical centre. Supported by such tangible and visible testimonies as the royal bronzes, it shines and will go on shining even beyond the boundaries of Africa as long as mankind exists.

Oni, the name by which Ife designates the almighty king, means 'he who possesses'. No Oni is allowed to bear his individual name and it is forbidden to utter this name of secular origin in designating a being who, henceforth, is considered superhuman. The Oni's government consisted of various categories of notables. First came the chiefs of the interior, that is to say of the palace; then, those of the exterior with control over the various city districts and adjacent areas; and, lastly, the noble servants of the king and his court. The enthronement of an Oni took place according to a very rigid and complicated protocol. As for the burial ceremony, let us quote Palau-Marti :

'Burial ceremonies are led by the first Omodewa (chief of the interior) and not by the Oni's close relatives whose role is confined to offering victims to the 201 theoretic *egbora** of Ife. The Omodewa, in turn, offer sacrifices outside the gates of the *afin**, in the presence of the crowd: sheep, goats and horses are the obligatory victims. Then comes the laying-out ceremony during which the Oni's body is washed with water from a special well; his head is shaved and both big toes tied together with a small metal chain specially made for the occasion. Lastly, his body is rubbed with a sort of chalk which comes from Benin, his neck is

DOGON. Door of sacred granary. Hardwood with dark patina, background of a lighter shade. The door consists of two small planks linked by wrought iron staples. Represents animal-symbols: hornbills, lizards, crocodiles, tortoises. The lock, also in wood, is surmounted by a man on horseback.

34   *Height: 37 cm.*   *Dogon (northern region, Mali Republic).*   *Maurice Nicaud Collection, Paris.*

adorned with necklaces and his body wrapped in a loin cloth. The deceased king is given the amulets he used to wear when alive, bead-decorated sandals are put on his feet and an *ade** on his head. The body lies in state in the *Lajodogun** (inside the afin), and the principal ade (the Oni has many of these head-dresses) and a sheep's tail are placed beside him. Then begins the procession of Ife notables headed by the chiefs of the interior who pay their last tribute to the king. The *Emewa**, who wear black loin cloths, approach backwards; when close to the Oni, they turn round and, in taking leave of the sovereign, lift their left leg, kneel, and, bowing down to the ground, pray for the king to join his earthly father when " crossing the border ".

' The chief carpenter chooses a fine iroko (*chlorophora excelsa.* Moraceae), cuts it down and makes from it some planks for the coffin. Before cutting down the tree he offers in sacrifice a he- and a she-goat and places a piece of white cloth at the foot of the tree trunk. While the coffin and tomb are being prepared, all noise in Ife ceases; when the silence is finally called off, the drums start, very softly at first, the keynote being given by the king's personal drum. The coffin is then laid near the tomb and the Oni's body, stretched out on the lid, is taken to the market place by eight *Emese** who, for about one hour, move to and fro amidst the worshipping crowd. The preparation of the tomb and the burial of the body are the responsibility of the Olokere, normally entrusted with the burial of suicides. The actual interment is very discreet; it takes place in the presence of only the Omodewa, the Emese, the Oranmiyan priests, a few close relatives of the Oni and a few Otu (these are boys carrying animals for sacrifice). The tomb is provided with a hole designed to receive the blood of animals which will be sacrificed later, and the king's drum, broken up into pieces, is laid upon the tomb together with a horse's skull. '

THE BENIN KINGDOM

A very large area on the western coast of Africa has long been known under the name of Benin. Probably it is the Benin bronze craft, one of the first to be known in Europe, which is responsible for this inaccurate geographic extension.

According to Landolphe, the city of Edo, formerly Benin City, was a stronghold:

' The city of Benin is as large as France's largest cities, with about eighty thousand inhabitants. It is surrounded by a ditch over twenty feet wide and as many feet deep. The earth removed from the ditch on the side of the town forms a bank planted with a thorny hedge so thick as to

DOGON. *Female ancestor figure with child. Hardwood with dark flaky patina. Strictly cylindrical in shape, with rhythmically interlocked forms, it is dominated by a meditative face similar to those which we admire in ancient Chinese sculptures and in Khmer statues.*
Height: 69 cm.   *Dogon (northern region, Mali Republic).*   *Private collection, Paris.*

preclude all passage even of animals. This high bank hides the houses from sight; they can be seen only on entering the city through one of the gates located at great intervals from each other.'

As a result of the British punitive expedition of 1897, the royal palace, which had occupied a large part of the city, was practically destroyed. In 1914, just before the First World War, King Eweka II had the palace rebuilt according to the original plans, but a fire destroyed a large part of it a few years later. Today, in spite of its precarious condition, it remains the largest group of buildings in the city, with some two hundred rooms and immense courtyards. When the kingdom was flourishing, the site was truly splendid. Let us quote David Van Nyendael who describes it in great detail in Bosman's *Description of the Coast of Guinea* published in Utrecht in 1704:

'The King's Court, which makes a principal Part of the City, must not be forgotten. It is upon a very great Plain, about which are no Houses, and hath, besides its wide Extent, nothing rare. The first Place we come into, is, a very long Gallery, if it must have that Name, which is sustained by fifty eight strong Planks, about twelve Foot high, instead of Pillars; these are neither saw'd nor plain'd, but only hack'd out. As soon as we are past this Gallery we come to the Mud or Earthern Wall, which hath three Gates, at each Corner one, and another in the Middle, the last of which is adorn'd at the top with a wooden Turret, like a Chimney, about sixty or seventy Foot high. At the top of all is fixed a large Copper Snake, whose Head hangs downwards: this Serpent is very well cast or carved, and is the finest I have seen in *Benin*. Entring one of these Gates we come into a plain about a quarter of a Mile, almost square, and enclosed with a low Wall. Being come to the end of this Plain, we meet with such another Gallery as the first, except that it hath neither Wall nor Turret. Some time since this Gallery was half thrown down by Thunder, since which no Hand hath been laid to it to re-build it. This Gallery hath a Gate at each End; and passing thro' one of them a third Gallery offers its self to view, differing from the former only in that the Planks upon which it rests are Humane Figures; but so wretchedly carved, that it is hardly possible to distinguish whether they are most like Men or Beasts; notwithstanding which my Guides were able to distinguish them into Merchants, Soldiers, Wild-Beast-Hunters, etc. Behind a white Carpet we are also shewn eleven Mens Heads cast in Copper, by much as good an Artist as the former Carvers and upon each of these is an Elephant's Tooth, these being some of the King's Gods. Going thro' a Gate of this Gallery we enter another great Plain and a fourth Gallery, beyond which is the King's Dwelling-House. Here is another Snake, as upon the first Wall. In the first Apartment at the entrance of the Plain, is the King's Audience-Chamber, where, in the presence of his three

DOGON. Mask in light wood. Stylisation of the mythical hare with hollowed-out beak-nose, surmounted by three kneeling female ancestor figures. Dark brown patina, contrasting with triangles whitewashed with kaolin. Height: 83 cm. *Dogon (northern region, Mali Republic).* *Henri Kamer Collection, Paris.*

38

Great Lords, I saw and spoke with him: He was sitting on an Ivory Couch under a Canopy of *Indian* Silk.

'He was a Person of an affable Mien, and about forty Years old. There was no Person in the Hall besides the three mentioned Great Lords, the King and a *Negroe* with a drawn Sword in his Hand, that look'd as fierce as a Cabin Centry. Whatever any Person would say to the King, must be first told to these Three, who then report it to him, and bring his Answer, going thus continually to and from him, without any Person's being able to determine whether they faithfully report the Messages on either side.

'On the King's left Hand, against a fine Tapestry, I saw seven white scoured Elephants Teeth on Pedestals of Ivory, which is the manner that all the King's Gods are placed within his House.'

A royal funeral gives rise to dramatic scenes. Landolphe, quoted above, gives us the following account:

'When the king of Benin dies, a hole is dug in one of the large courtyards of the palace, four feet square on top, thirty feet deep and much wider at the bottom. The king is lowered into this hole together with his chief ministers — the latter alive — and the hole is covered with a large wooden trap-door. Food is carried there daily and the people ask if the king is dead, to which the wretched creatures answer that he is very ill. This goes on until there is no answer — needless to say, the ministers too have died. Thereupon, for a few days, the city is in mourning. Masked men wearing gigantic costumes and armed with a *damas* (sword) go through the streets, chopping off the heads of those whom they encounter, collecting the blood in copper basins and pouring it out on to the king's tomb. Eventually, the bodies of the king and his ministers are removed from the hole, and the victims are returned to their families who bury them inside their houses. The king is buried in a wide courtyard under a spacious porch supported by twelve large pillars representing tall men of great rank.

'In examining one of these tombs, I noticed many elephant tusks of a dazzling whiteness, seven feet long. It was dreadful, however, to see this place soaked in human blood. On the cover of the tomb there was a snake made of tusks skilfully jointed together; thirty feet long and six feet round the middle, its mouth open, its tongue represented by a copper blade, it seemed to glide down from the top of the cover as if worming its way into the tomb.'

The carved ivories and brass plates decorating the pillars and walls of the palace often represent the Oba with his arms outstretched and supported by two figures as if he were incapable of

KURUMBA. Stylised antelope. Light wood decorated with triangular sections sprinkled with white dots. Like the Bambara ' chi wara ', this sculpture has its female counterpart. In the oldest examples, like this one, the tips of the ears are joined to the very straight horns.

40   *Height: 110 cm.*   *Kurumba (Upper-Volta Republic).*   *Faculty of Letters, Strasbourg.*

sustaining alone his limbs laden with bracelets. A description by Burton, published in 1864, corroborates this testimony and certifies its historical authenticity. Without giving us any explanation, the works cast in bronze reveal to us the association between the Oba and certain animals with which he is generally represented, especially the panther and the snake. Several European museums still have in their collections snake heads made of bronze, the bodies of which have disappeared.

DAHOMEY

A link can be traced between the Fon country and the large Yoruba kingdom. The history of Dahomey focuses on that of the Abomey kingdom, capital of the Fon. Although there have been other kingdoms, they have sunk into oblivion and vanished, overpowered by the splendour and radiance of the Behanzin court and its successors, the Aho, who still survive. Dahomey originated with a dynasty of warriors who settled down in the Abomey plateau. The numerous smaller kingdoms nearby had to yield to King Agaja's power. According to tradition, the king's mythical ancestor was a male panther who had possessed the king's daughter while she was lost in the woods. She gave birth to a boy called Agasu who claimed the throne when he came of age. There have been many versions of this legend, and we might mention that the Negroes — and people of other continents as well — have a real craving for fabulous ancestors of mysterious origin. The Agasu myth ended up in an almost Christian version in which Agasu, according to Palau-Marti, was only ' the spiritual son of the panther, and was discovered by King Sado's wife like an infant Jesus in his crib '.

During the reign of Agaja from 1708 to 1730, Dahomey expanded along the coast and conquered Whydah and Alada, almost destroying the latter in 1727. From then on, the king of Abomey traded directly with the Europeans, all along the coast, without unnecessary and costly intermediaries. He created a special category of officials responsible for negotiations and trade. In most instances it was the king's son who succeeded to the throne, but sometimes a brother rather than a son inherited the throne of the deceased king. As in all countries of Yoruba ancestry, he who was designated king had to be of unblemished moral and physical character, and the slightest weakness deprived him of all rights to succession. After the famous reign of Agaja the Conqueror, Tegbesu came into power and reigned from 1732 to 1774. Travellers of those days report that Tegbesu was an affable king, clever in dealing with foreigners. Robert Norris gives an account of his visit to him in 1772:

' Having bowed to the king, I was directed to a chair a few yards from him; and having drank

BOBO. Large antelope mask with long curved horns, which enhance the inverted shape of the animal's head. Hardwood painted in red, yellow, black and white.
Height: 85 cm.   Bobo-Fing (Upper-Volta Republic).   Musée des Arts Africains et Océaniens, Paris.

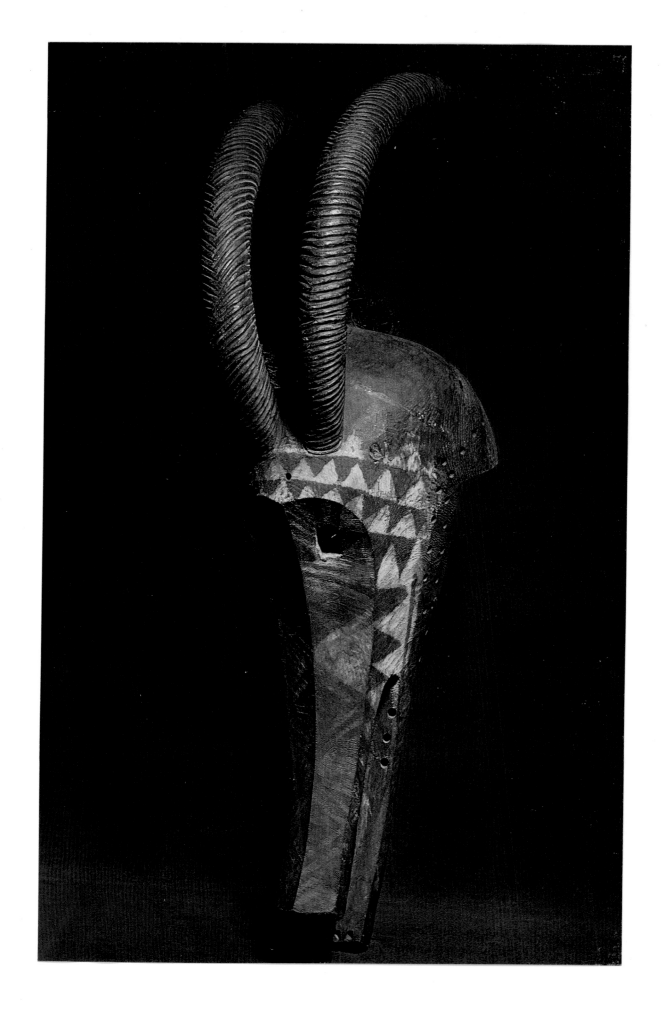

his health in a small glass of brandy, and he mine, he inquired after the health of his brother, *King George* of *England;* and asked some questions respecting my voyage... After some conversation he desired me to let him hear the organ, and appeared much pleased with the tunes. I then explained the use of the sedan chair, which I represented as much more convenient than hammocs, which he generally used. Half a dozen of his hammoc men were then introduced, crawling on their hands and knees; and by his desire, I went into the sedan, and directing them what to do, was carried by them all in turns, until they appeared to be pretty expert at their business: he then went into it himself, and was carried repeatedly round the court, amidst the shouts and acclamations of his ministers, his women, and his hammoc men. It was a smart, showy thing, covered with red morocco leather, and lined with white silk. He was astonishingly delighted with it, and diverted himself with opening and drawing the curtains, which he deemed a most ingenious contrivance; at last, in the exultation of his soul, some of the eunuchs were called in to supply the place of the hammoc men, and the door leading from the piazza to his private apartments being opened, he was carried by them to display his finery among his women; and I had permission to depart. '

The city of Abomey, situated on a large plateau, is very extensive, and the royal palace consists of several communicating square courtyards. Some distance away, there are the convents of the royal ' fetishes ' where young girls, consecrated to the river or thunder, are educated. Another courtyard is reserved for the king's wives, assembled in a sort of college and closely watched by the eldest of the royal princesses. Abomey means ' enclosed ', for the old city was fortified, surrounded by red earth walls, sections of which can still be seen, and by a large ditch. The kings' tombs are marked by small, circular temples with very low entrances. Small altars for the worship of ancestors are scattered around Abomey and nearby villages; iron and copper objects called *asen*, resembling the framework of an umbrella, are related to this practice and are the object of regular sacrifices and worship. Certain historical emotions can be experienced — even in Africa — only in the silence of a museum; neither living legends nor living customs can arouse them. The large thrones and *recados* of the Abomey museum are eloquent. Cut from a single trunk of soft wood, with perforated shafts, these royal seats are similar in style to those of the Ashanti. Actually, most of them are replicas of ancient thrones, the originals having been destroyed by the fire which broke out in the royal palace during the Behanzin rout. Some of them are supported by the skulls of four defeated enemies. The *recados* which kings and dignitaries carried on their shoulders consist of a wooden handle at the end of which is inserted a piece resembling

BOBO. Large ' Molo' mask, a Bobo-Fing representation of divinity. Very hard dense wood with an inner patina indicating long use. Face with human features surmounted by wonderfully carved horns which give the appearance of the natural material, in spite of their deliberate stylisation. The goatee beard, typical of Bobo masks, appears under the mouth. Red, black and white geometrical decorations, black horns.

Height: 140 cm.   Bobo-Fing (Upper-Volta Republic).   Musée des Arts Africains et Océaniens, Paris.

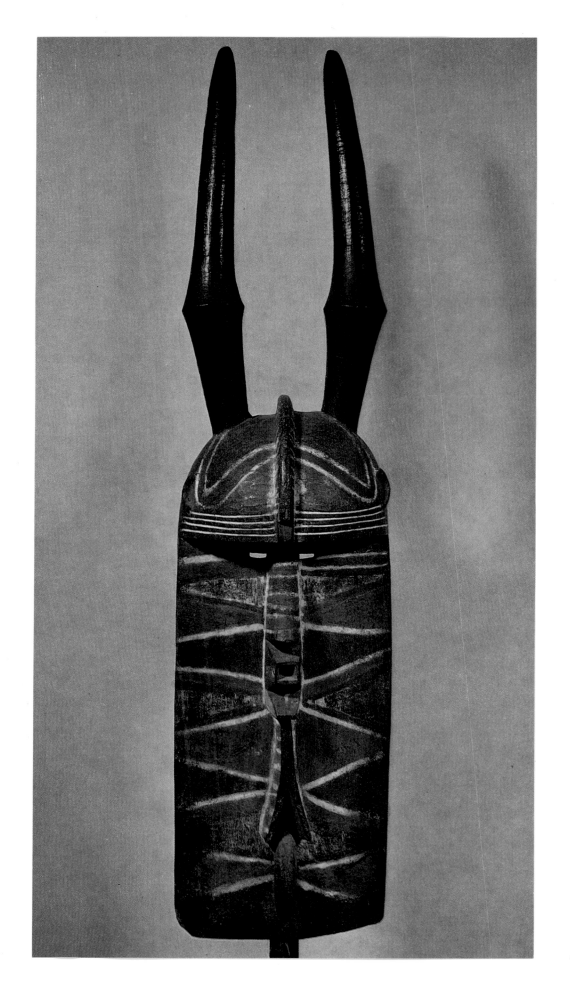

45

an axe-head, usually of metal but sometimes of ivory, decorated with animals or symbols; directly descended from the war-club — the classical weapon before the appearance of firearms — they symbolise power and dignity. Incidentally, one of the peoples to the north of Dahomey, the Somba, still live by hunting, using bow and arrow with great skill.

THE GOLD COAST — ASHANTI

In the seventeenth and eighteenth centuries, gold and slaves were the main exports of this country which was already known as the Gold Coast. A British traveller, Bowdich, gives us the following account of his visit to the king of Ashanti at the beginning of the last century:

'He wore a fillet of *aggry** beads round his temples, a necklace of gold cockspur-shells strung by their largest ends, and over his right shoulder a red silk cord, suspending three Saphies — Moslem amulets — cased in gold; his bracelets were the richest mixtures of beads and gold, and his fingers covered with rings; his cloth was of a dark green silk; a pointed diadem was elegantly painted in white on his forehead; also a pattern resembling an epaulette on each shoulder, and an ornament like a full-blown rose, one leaf rising above another until it covered his whole breast; his knee-bands were of aggry beads, and his ankle-strings of gold ornaments of the most delicate workmanship, small drums, sankos, stools, swords, guns, and birds, clustered together; his sandals, of a soft white leather, were embossed across the instep-band with small gold and silver cases of saphies; he was seated in a low chair, richly ornamented with gold; he wore a pair of gold castanets on his finger and thumb, which he clapped to enforce silence. The belts of the guards behind his chair were cased in gold, and covered with small jaw-bones of the same metal; the elephant's tails, waving like a small cloud before him, were spangled with gold, and large plumes of feathers were flourished amid them. His eunuch presided over these attendants, wearing only one massy piece of gold about his neck: the royal stool, entirely cased in gold, was displayed under a splendid umbrella, with drums, sankos, horns, and various musical instruments, cased in gold, about the thickness of cartridge paper: large circles of gold hung by scarlet cloth from the swords of state, the sheaths as well as the handles of which were also cased; hatchets of the same were intermixed with them: the breasts of the *Ocrahs** and various attendants were adorned with large stars, stools, crescents, and gossamer wings of solid gold. '

Apparently, we must take Bowdich's word for the accuracy of his lavish report. However, in spite of his obvious desire to dazzle the reader, it may be worthwhile to compare his statements

MARKA. Mask in hardwood covered with repoussé brass plating. Upright female figure between the two horns. From a neighbouring tribe of the Bambara, it still retains the characteristics of an individual style. Height: 74 cm. Marka (south-east frontier region, Mali Republic). Pierre Vérité Collection, Paris.

47

with objects that can be seen in the British Museum and elsewhere, and that seem to correspond, after all, to his report: Some of the breast decorations and other royal insignia are on exhibition in the British Museum. The low chair — or one very like it — can be seen at Accra; instead of castanets, there are silver bells — undoubtedly used for the same purpose — hanging on either side. As for the ceremonial swords, they are still to be found among the Baule and the Ashanti; they are made of wood and covered with a very thin gold plate stuck on with egg paste — a method used by our framers for leaf-gilding and our book-binders for ' stamping '.

KINGDOM OF CONGO

At the end of the fifteenth century, the Portuguese Diogo Cão came by sea to the estuary of a large river which divided a huge state, later called Congo. It was difficult to determine the exact boundaries of this kingdom or even empire, though it consisted of large and distinct provinces, some of which retain to this day a very individual style: coastal Loango, Kakongo and Nyogo and, lastly, Angola which the same Diogo Cão visited around 1483.

As a result of Portuguese missionary activity in Congo, King Manikongo was converted to Christianity and accepted it wholeheartedly; he was the first of this new dynasty to reign under his Christian name, Affonso I. During this period, many art objects both sacred and secular were brought in from Portugal; these greatly influenced the sculpture of these countries: relatively recent Bakongo representations of motherhood still call to mind the Madonna and Child, while the free variations of the *Holo** panels are faintly reminiscent of the theme of the Crucifixion.

LOBI. Head in hardwood with brown patina. This illustrates an old and obsolete custom in which the person was made to wear in his upper lip a quartz lip-plug or labret. The north Dahomey Somba frequently still wear such discs in their ear lobes.

Height: 23 cm.   Lobi (southern region, Upper-Volta Republic).   M. Komor Collection, New York.

49

Later, the sixteenth and especially the early seventeenth century marks the beginning of the decline of central authority, a decline similar to that of the great Benin kingdom in the eighteenth century. About 1717, Christianity was rejected and its European representatives driven out. Though animism gradually resumed its sway, the memory of Christian forms survived; holy images were merely transformed into fetishes. The word 'fetish' has been so often misused to describe objects and sculptures in Negro Africa, that we think it advisable to state what is known of its etymology. Some interpret the Portuguese word 'feticio' to mean something 'factitious'; others feel it refers to a hollow object, whether natural or man-made, filled with magic substance, loaded with 'invisible' physical power. In fact, any primitive sculpture was classified as a 'fetish'. Now we know that the term fetish applies to a limited number of objects considered locally as dangerous, their power proceeding from that of the sorcerer-maker. Most negro initiation masks, funeral reliquaries and spell-casting divinities contain beneficial magic power. They help man to achieve a harmonious integration with the world; they help both the earth and the animals to continue to provide food for man in the great cycle of life.

To conclude this brief historical outline which brings us to the close of the last century, let us mention the foundation, in 1885, of the Congo state under Belgian control. Leopoldville became the capital of the country, an administrative and business centre. The administrative authorities obeyed strict orders and methodically assembled numerous objects of the most varied styles : according to Maesen, about one hundred, including sub-styles.

This research work, the most systematic to have been carried out at a time when many colonising countries showed but little interest in this art, enabled Belgium to set up a Royal Museum, at Tervuren near Brussels, perhaps the richest in the world with reference to a single ethnic group. It is admired by art lovers and provides a wide field of study for research workers.

In the central Congo, the Bakuba claim 124 kings of divine lineage. The name Bakuba means 'men of lightning'. It is assumed that this race invaded the Upper Ubangi region during the first thousand years AD. Tradition tells of the migration of these people, of their subsequent crossing of four large watercourses, and of the rather light complexion of their kings. They are said to have settled in Sankuru around the sixth century, under the reign of Minga Bengale, sixth king of this dynasty. The Bakuba empire was at its height at the beginning of the seventeenth century, under Shamba Bolongongo, a peace- and civilisation-loving sovereign. He was a philosopher as well as a moralist and is frequently cited as an example of great humanity despite his 'divine essence'. He was the first to attach importance to art. He established the custom — strictly complied with ever since — of having the royal effigies carved in very hard wood, nineteen of which survive in museums.

DAN. Wooden mask with coffee-coloured patina. Badly eroded, it is impressive in spite of the softness of its forms. The eyes, almost closed, are surrounded by a whitened linear frame.
Height: 23 cm. Dan-Yakuba (Ivory Coast, western frontier). Private collection, Paris.

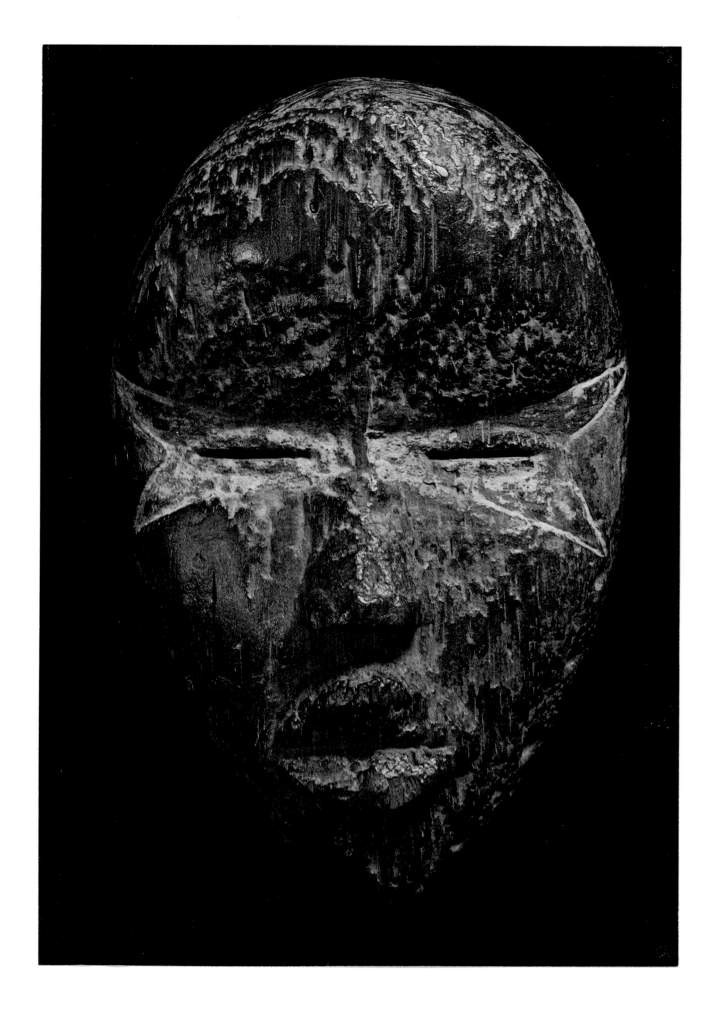

MATERIALS AND TECHNIQUES

TERRACOTTA

Though it is difficult to determine when terracotta made its first appearance in any part of the globe, it is reasonable to assume that it followed soon after the discovery of fire: the formation of hard layers under domestic hearths and on the soil must have intrigued our forefathers. With the exception, of course, of the ice-cap areas, excavations have brought to light pieces of broken pottery all over the world. As for Africa — with which we are here concerned — one of the oldest (probably 2000-1700 BC) as well as finest examples known, is undoubtedly the small figure of a woman from Aniba (Nubia), discovered in the course of excavations sponsored by Cairo University in 1962. Beautiful vases with human and floral decorations were found in the same site and during the same excavations (1960-3). Outstanding relics of high quality also include the Nok heads; unfortunately, many of them were destroyed during early investigations. There is no doubt, however, that African archaeology which was still toddling at the beginning of the century, has now attained childhood and even adolescence. Thanks to Bernard Fagg, J.-P. Lebeuf, Henri Lhote, Lajoux and a few others, we may look forward hopefully to the next few years. The Nok sculptures are dated to the last 300 years BC. While the firing of this pottery is far from perfect, the heads of the Ife queens which we were able to examine at close quarters seem to have been moulded in a finer (or better crushed?) clay and baked at a higher temperature. May we infer from this that the Ife artists, so skilful in casting brass, had built radiation furnaces? In any case, apart from this islet of perfection, we must admit that most of the ancient Krinjabo funeral figures from the south-west Ivory Coast do not reach the artistic level attained by other African groups, and that their sculptures and vases in clay are extremely fragile and few have remained intact.

The scarified head in the La Rochelle Museum (see page 107) seems to be very hard: the Sao must have used high-temperature furnaces.

On the Ivory Coast, in the heart of the Baule country, the pottery centre of Kotiola produces large quantities of jars of all shapes and for all purposes; the craftsmen find on the spot good quality clay spangled with mica-schist, of a light-yellow shade which, when baked, becomes a beautiful shade of red. Unfortunately, these jars are very fragile. Many workshops have been

DAN. Mask in hard and polished wood with red highlights. Hair and plaits in animal fibre or hair. The pursuit of beauty through the regularity and tension of lines and volumes is here obvious.

52   *Height: 30 cm.*   *Dan-Yakuba (Ivory Coast, western frontier).*   *Maurice Nicaud Collection, Paris.*

set up in the largest centres to reproduce ancient models and to satisfy the increasing demands of tourists. However, to insist on systematically perpetuating a tradition which is no longer a living one resembles the efforts of a surgeon trying to avoid amputation of a gangrenous limb. The history of art has taught us that the only way to progress is to turn away from the past, to slam the door in its face — besides, the influence of the past is strong enough to persist in spite of our turning away from it.

STONE

Although stone is present throughout Negro Africa, only a few varieties are suitable for sculpture. This may account for the limited number of stone sculptures in Africa. Laterite, similar in appearance to the French millstone grit, is quite unsuitable for cutting. In Kissi, Guinea, Sherbro and even Sierra Leone, the statuettes and funeral heads are made of steatite (soapstone), which is so soft that it can be cut with a pocket knife. This accounts for the erosion of ancient relics, and should serve to warn the amateur against any works which have clear, sharp details, even though our knowledge of the styles of different periods makes fraud rather difficult. The same material is used a long way off, by the Bakongo, where pensive-looking funeral figures have been found in attitudes of supreme detachment, the head usually resting on one hand and the legs crossed (one raised above the other). Many more

DAN. Statuette of a woman carrying her child on her back. It is soft wood with a black patina; the eyes are emphasised by a light pattern, as on the dance masks. This is one of the very rare examples of the mother and child theme in Dan sculpture.
Height: 64 cm.   Dan-Yakuba (Ivory Coast, western frontier).   Musée des Arts Africains et Océaniens, Paris.

sculptures, of which the birds are the most famous, have been found as far down as Rhodesia and Zimbabwe itself; here again, the stone is a type of soapstone similar to that used in Guinea and Congo. An analysis of the famous 'bird-man' in the Tishman collection has revealed that it is made of a much harder material — a sort of dark-green basalt. Certainly the largest collection of stone sculptures — over eight hundred — is at Esie in the north of the Yoruba country; it includes masterpieces of expressiveness and poise. Here again, the material used is mainly soapstone.

The Ekoi group of ancestral figures, recently described by Philip Allison, consists of about three hundred large monoliths planted in the ground. These are made of a very hard material — granite or basalt.

Finally, quartz has been used at Ife to carve thrones; this, however, is the only example of its use in Africa.

WOOD

There are several reasons why wood is the material most often used by the craftsmen of Negro Africa. First of all, it is found throughout the forest areas. In the savannah it is scarcer though even there it exists in sufficient quantity to satisfy the requirements of building and sculpture. Secondly, and this is perhaps the more important factor, we know that no African undertaking is entirely free and gratuitous, and since wood is a living material, it is felt that the masks and statuettes derive their magical power from the branch or trunk of a tree whose roots drew nourishment from the earth and whose leaves received water from the sky. Such a process is not so much sculpture as the transmutation of power through the modification of form.

In the Sudanese grasslands, for example, the carpenter-sculptor goes into spiritual and physical retirement (isolation, meditation, chastity) before setting out to carve a mask or the image of a mythical ancestor. He implores the tree to forgive him the removal of one of its branches, and only then begins his task. The African carving technique is so simple and at the same time powerful that one can only wonder at the results, considering the rudimentary tools used: the hatchet, a sort of small axe with a rounded blade at one end used to rough-hew the main planes and successive volumes of the proposed work, and the adze, also a small axe with the cutting edge at right angles to the handle. These rudimentary tools are practically the only ones used throughout Negro Africa. Yet, they succeed in producing dynamic works of sculpture. The Baluba, known for their refinement, turn these implements into trade insignia: the handle is fashioned in the shape of a human being, whose head appears to spit out the metal blade.

One of the later steps is the carving of details by means of a short knife held well into the

NGERE-WOBE. Mask called Gla* in blackened wood surrounded by bells, seeds, cartridges and compact masses of miscellaneous origin. (The wheel of a clock can be seen above the right ear.)
Height: 36 cm.   *Ngere-Wobe (Ivory Coast, western frontier).*   *Private collection, Paris.*

56

hand. Polishing, sometimes of very high quality, is accomplished by using leaves with an abrasive surface. The final step is the ritual decoration of masks and statues. Soft wood, such as bombax or kapok-tree wood, does not stand an oily, transparent patina; consequently, especially in the savannah area, wood is painted, often in very bright colours having a precise ritual meaning. Other masks in soft wood, those for example of the Kono society (or other secret societies on the Liberia - Ivory Coast border) are first covered with a sort of blackish glue made of animal blood, natural black dye and oil, which acts as a fixative. Actually, this fixing is rather precarious, for the surface often peels off. As for hardwood, it is interesting to note that the ebony tree is never used for ritual carving but only for commercial purposes. A number of Baule, Guro and Yaure masks, some statuettes of the same style, numerous Baluba statues, the famous Bakuba kings series and countless other carvings are made in hardwood, similar to mahogany in solidity and grain, the colour varying from red to dark brown and sometimes, but seldom, to light yellow. Of course this type of wood (Makore) requires and withstands a finer finish and a more thorough polish than does softwood, while the beauty of the material is not shown to advantage if the wood is painted; sometimes, it is dyed with the juice of red seeds from a local bush, as for example the beautiful Guro mask (page 73) carved in such a hardwood. Patina, currently called weathering, improves with time, and the craftsman takes that fact into account from the very start. The expressive parts of the face — forehead, eyes, nose and mouth — are given special attention; here, patina is obtained by using palm-tree oil which gives beautiful orange highlights.

IRON

Iron was used many hundreds of years before the Christian era in the region where the present-day Sudan is located. Iron probably came from Nubia and spread well beyond the Sudanese area; we find relics of it throughout Negro Africa. We have already stressed the important role played by smiths in African societies, and it is to be expected that their forged and hammered works should be held in general esteem. The technique is a simple one (the red-hot iron bar is forged on the anvil) and has not changed for centuries, the skill lying in the stroke of the hammer.

The Bambara iron votive poles planted in the earth deserve special mention: they feature either a horseman or a woman, a motherly goddess seated in an attitude of remote dignity, similar to the Buguni wooden queens.

The Dogon show great inventiveness in representing animals in wrought iron; the Bakuba-

BAULE. Door of hut in reddened wood, the reverse side strongly weathered by smoke. Helmeted horseman and the bird known as the 'ox-pecker' on the horse's croup. On the right, a crocodile devouring a fish.
Height: 135 cm.   Baule (Ivory Coast, central region).   Musée des Arts Africains et Océaniens, Paris.

Bushongo wrought ironwork is famous in the Congo. Even a king of the great dynasty devoted his time to this craft and there is a sculpture representing him with an anvil at his feet. In Nigeria, at Ise, in the south of Etiki, there are many of these iron poles planted in the earth and decorated with groups of birds, the largest bird perched on top of the pole. This is one of the many examples of the originality and inventiveness of African sculptors.

Reference is made in this book to the powerful Bukoba bull now at Stuttgart (page 216 *top*); apart from the amazing artistic conception, it is, in all its bareness, an example of remarkable technique with perfect curves and smoothly polished surface.

BRONZE

The technique of casting bronze or any other alloy, easily analysed today, has been often described, though not always accurately. Except for some improvements due to industrial progress and to certain 'tricks' of the trade, this technique known as *cire perdue* or 'lost-wax' has not changed for centuries. In order to understand the method used by the Ife, Benin, Ivory Coast and Baule founders, one might begin by reading Benvenuto Cellini's lively description of this craft in his autobiography, and one might then visit the studios of, say, Georges Rudier at Châtillon-sous-Bagneux. Rudier is responsible for the preservation of sculptures by Rodin, Bourdelle, Maillol, Arp, Adam and a few other great modern sculptors. We shall see, to start with, that brass casting is a dramatic venture, actually a second creation, for a cast that comes flawless out of the mould is a success preceded by no little apprehension, whether it measures ten centimetres or two metres. The sculptor begins by shaping the wax, softening it by moulding it, or exposing it to a source of heat, sun or fire. If the sculpture is large and must be cast hollow (as is usually the case), he prepares a core, that is to say the reduced but fairly accurate shape of the proposed sculpture; to do so he uses rather hard clay (thus avoiding contraction) mixed with bits of crushed straw and sand or silica to make it porous and at the same time solid. Then he coats the core with softened wax, giving the work its final shape and bringing out the details, always bearing in mind that 'wax is equal to metal' and that the more even the thickness of the wax, the better the chance of the mould coming uncracked and flawless. Two wax rods joined to a lump of wax are added to the bottom of the wax mould (though not at Ife); these form the pouring cup and vents for the entry of the molten metal and the escape of air and gases. The artist's task is followed by that of the founder who coats the sculpture with a first thin layer of very fine-grain clay in solution, usually extracted from the inner galleries of termitaries: this material — easily handled and capable of great precision — reproduces all the subtleties of the wax form,

BAULE. Ancestor mask in natural wood. The face expresses deep concentration and is topped with three wooden stalks which do not resemble the combs of this type of mask.
Height: 39 cm.   Baule (Ivory Coast, central region).   Henri Kamer Collection, Cannes.

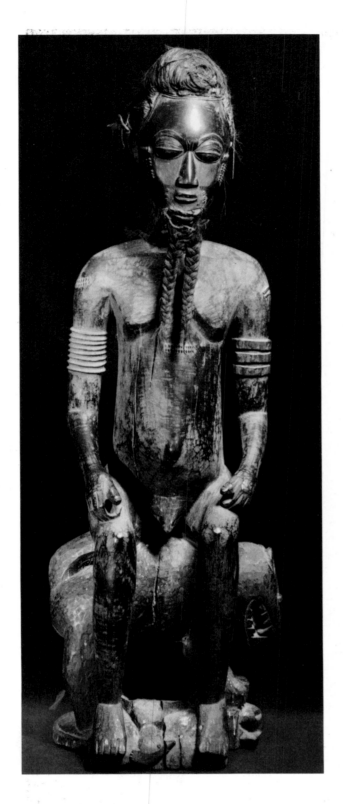

even to the artist's fingerprints; subsequent layers of clay are added to a thickness of one or two inches. When the clay is set, the founder fixes the external casing to the core by means of iron nails so as to keep the core in its place once the wax has disappeared. The complete mould thus obtained is put to dry in a ventilated but shady place to avoid cracks and splits which might mar the cast. When completely dry, the sculpture is fired upside down in the furnace and the wax burned out in vapour. The empty mould is then buried in a sort of hole, head downwards, and surrounded by packed earth, leaving a double vent for the outflow.

The African craftsman uses his goat-skin bellows to heat the required amount of metal in his crucible; when the metal is liquid, he pours it into the mould until it overflows slightly through one of the vent-holes. The subsequent operations are simpler: the cold mould is extracted and broken, the broken-up core is cleaned from the inside of the cast. The last steps are chiselling, polishing and producing a patina. All these operations are necessary to make the finished work durable, if not beautiful.

The best-known African bronzes are the Ife heads, discovered in the course of many excavations. There are only eighteen of these. Apart from their plastic beauty, they are considered the summit of metal craftsmanship in Negro Africa because of their technical perfection — especially the even thickness of the metal.

BAULE. Ancestor statue. In blackened wood with a shiny patina, and with natural hair and beard. The statue, with numerous groovings, represents an old man seated on an animal whose eyes are made of fragments of yellow glass, probably a leopard, with a dead cock lying among its feet, and another dead animal under its paws. Height: 100 cm. Baule (Ivory Coast, central region). Pierre Vérité Collection, Paris.

63

Then there are the Jebba archer and the bronze statues (including the seated figure at the island of Tada), the largest found in Africa to date. The flawless brass-casting technique is further exemplified by the numerous Benin brass plaques, the heads of queen-mothers, the aqua-maniles in the shape of panthers or rams, the horsemen, and the famous throne, now at the Dahlem Museum in Berlin, of which the Nigerian museums also have a similar specimen.

In the Cameroons, the Bamum and Bali are skilful founders, and we know of beautiful masks and cleverly shaped ceremonial pipes. We shall not dwell on Dahomey craftsmanship which, though technically praiseworthy, is of no great artistic value.

The *Kuduo** funeral receptacles of the Ashanti are of very elaborately worked brass, beautifully cast; the most ancient ones are the finest. The numerous goldweights, the human and animal-shaped masks (often illustrating proverbs) testify to the Ashanti mastery of the *cire perdue,* or lost-wax technique described above. Their neighbours, the Baule, when emigrating to the Ivory Coast, brought this technique with them and transmitted this passion for metal to their northern and western neighbours, the Senufo and the Yakuba. The latter produce delicate and beautifully moulded small 'reference' masks, probably intended to fix the style in a stable material. The Abidjan Museum has many remarkable specimens with a green patina, called 'excavation bronzes'. Bronze cups, worthy of the highest civilisation, have been found among the Sao of the Chad area, but so far there has been no trace of anthropomorphous metal statuettes. Our information is of course incomplete, but so far there is no evidence of bronze craft in the region extending from the Gaboon to the Congo, the Bantu countries and Rhodesia. Perhaps future archaeologists will prove differently.

GOLD

To obtain gold, the Africans rely almost entirely on the gold-washing process, by means of which gold-bearing earth, gathered from the river- and stream-beds, is panned. We cannot possibly list here all the sites which have been explored and eventually abandoned. The exploitation of such sites was a job for the individual craftsman; it involves little expenditure and makes use of low-grade soil.

History teaches us that much of the royal metal used in Egypt came from Negro Africa.

The main sources of production are the Chad area, Upper Sudan, north Dahomey, along the Cavally on the Ivory Coast, the Gold Coast (present-day Ghana), Guinea and many other sites it would be tedious to list. All sorts of African works were cast in gold, especially those designed for kings and notables, but few have remained and those which have are very small in size.

BAULE. Double mask with different patina for each face: red under a dark crust for the female, smooth and shiny brown for the male. Made in hardwood.

Height: 27.5 cm.   Baule (Ivory Coast, central region).   Henri Kamer Collection, Cannes.

The Wallace Collection in London has an Ashanti head, probably a funeral effigy mask. If we are to credit traveller's reports, the Ashanti produced a large quantity of works of this type. It is regrettable that most of these masterpieces have been recast into ingots and used as money in the course of wars, conquests and revolutions.

In the British Museum and at Accra, there are still fine collections of breast ornaments and royal head-gear with gold appliqué, either treated with the *cire perdue* process or in very finely embossed plating — a solar art drawing inspiration from plant life and rarely from human shape. Small masks featuring the faces of defeated warriors have been found in great numbers on the Ivory Coast among chiefdoms of the Akan group (Baule, Attie, Agni). The technique used in casting these pendants, masks, insignia and ornamental plates of Ashanti or Baule origin is very much the same as the brass casting technique, except that the wax is sometimes treated differently: many of these masterpieces are made up of small waxen threads, the size of a Chinese noodle, rolled up on a wooden plate and stuck together side by side according to the overall form of the work which then assumes a streaked, vibrating appearance. Incidentally, A. Pevsner has very successfully resorted to the welding of parallel copper wires in his monumental modern sculptures.

Working with gold is easier than working with bronze in that gold sculpture does not require a ' suspended ' core but merely a suitable filling supporting the original model, but this is only because the castings in gold are considerably smaller.

IVORY

It may be surprising that, despite the enormous amount of ivory produced by Negro Africa for centuries and the durability of this material, so few ancient works in ivory have survived. Actually, the explanation is simple enough: ivory and gold were the main items of trade, first with Egypt, then, from the sixteenth century onwards or even earlier, with Europe. Moreover, with the exception of a few specimens, African sculpture was not valued. Consequently, ivory was exported as raw material, first by caravan and later by ship. It would be interesting — if it were possible — to determine the origin of the tusks in which our Gothic virgins were carved. We know that the tusks of Asian elephants are much smaller than those of their African cousins. The latter can measure as much as two metres, and the average size of tusks normally sold by the West African forestry service is one and a half metres (about 5 feet).

The technique of carving ivory is very similar to that of carving wood, both materials having a ' grain ' that must be respected, if parts of the work are not to crack. Ivory is harder than the

BAULE. Ancestor mask topped with a toucan. In hardwood with an extremely smooth patina which looks almost lacquered, with yellow and red-brown highlights. The triangular face with nearly-closed heavy eyelids gives the impression of deep concentration and peaceful meditation, symbol of wisdom attained. Height: 40 cm.   Baule (Ivory Coast, central region).   Private collection, Paris.

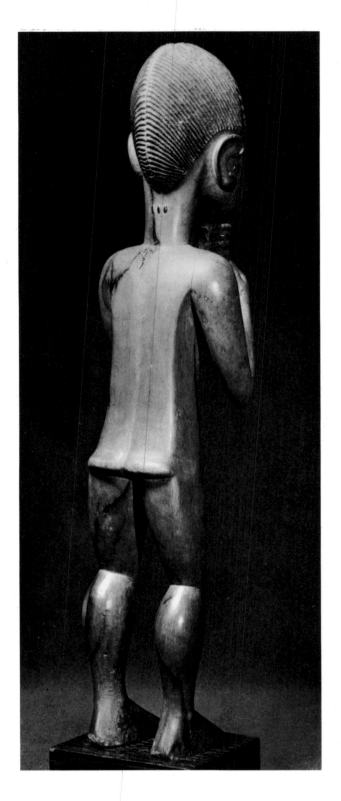

hardest of woods and, therefore, the tools have to be re-sharpened frequently.

When we examine the salt-cellars and spoons, these little masterpieces of Afro-Portuguese art, which must be included in a discussion of African art even though they were undoubtedly made to order, and when we observe their finish and polish, we recognise that they called for a set of extremely precise tools which the Africans had to invent. They almost certainly had to invent a sort of 'perforator' for fretwork (unless they obtained such an instrument from Europe).

Let us list briefly the most outstanding carvings of African ethnic origin: the Attie (Ivory Coast) combs decorated with faces and even crucified figures; the beautifully carved Baule fly-whisks and fan-handles reminiscent of Romanesque capitals; the royal Dahomey *recados* partly in perforated ivory; and, from as far as Keitu, near the Nigerian border, the small carved horns for the worship of *Fa**. The fine Owo statuettes produced by the Yoruba are unfortunately very rare; one of them is in the Pitt-Rivers Museum, Oxford. In Central Nigeria, the Bini were undoubtedly the largest producers of ivory work: royal masks, the brow surrounded by heads; large royal panthers inlaid with bronze nails, and lastly, the famous 'historical' tusks. Central Congo abounds in small ivories: insignia, small masks, amulets, call-up horns, etc. Most of the Baluba, Bapende and Warega relics are admirable both in shape and patina.

BAULE. Small ancestor statuette in light wood with smooth patina. One hesitates to apply the word ancestor to this charming sculpture which gives the impression of youth. But the notion of ancestor, purely symbolic in African art, does not imply decay, wrinkles and decrepitude.
Height: 38 cm.   *Baule (Ivory Coast, central region).*   *Henri Kamer Collection, Cannes.*

STYLES

GUINEA

In the Bissagos Islands, off Portuguese Guinea, the Bidjogo, a fishing people, produce primitive female statuettes intended to favour marriage and conception. But their art rises to great heights, both in spirit and form, in the animal masks — wild bulls and oxen — with multicoloured decorations and real horns (see page 9). These terrifying masks are often attached to the bows of their canoes.

The Baga — an agricultural and fishing people on the coast of what was formerly French Guinea — are renowned for some of their sculptures. However, the variety and richness of their art has not been fully explored. The large face of the bird-man which we reproduce on page 13 is undoubtedly the only representation of the supreme Baga god. It is kept in a secret place, out of sight of the uninitiated, and taken out with great pomp every seven years during the dry season, when it is planted in a rice-field bordering on the village. During the period of initiation the young men must make their way to it between two rows of men armed with sticks. Having touched the god, they must return along the same dangerous passage where they are cudgelled; only then are they considered to have reached manhood.

The other representations of divine spirits, called Axiol or Attiol, marvels of technique, are merely permanent delegates of the supreme god, which always remain in the villages.

The snake Bandjoni is also a divine representative born of water and earth. It has been and still is used by the police to trace thieves and recover lost objects. Its services are acknowledged by offerings in kind.

The Baga attain a very high artistic level in sculpture which may be considered monumental when compared with the usually smaller African works. We reproduce on page 11 the rare specimen of a drum, very similar to the one kept at the British Museum. Judging by the style and technique, they are the work of one and the same sculptor, who was certainly a master. A comparison with Catalan Romanesque sculpture is unavoidable and perhaps not unreasonable: the

GURO. Mask representing a human face, gaunt, surmounted and surrounded by the horns of a gazelle, or perhaps a coiffure with plaits. In hardwood, shiny through use. The face is light, the coiffure darker. The elongated purity of form is typical of this style, related to that of the Baule.
Height: 42 cm.   *Guro (Ivory Coast, central region).*   *Olivier Le Corneur Collection, Paris.*

presentation of the child by its mother seems of Christian inspiration, and only the small drum is linked to African tradition. According to Maurice Nicaud there are few drum sculptors among the Baga.

It may be that the sculptures inspired by the mother-and-child theme and the large horse carrying a big drum (of which a fine specimen is kept at the Musée des Arts Africains et Océaniens, Paris, and another at the Joseph Muller Collection, Solothurn) are of similar if not identical origin.

The large *nimba* masks (page 137) are another example of monumental sculpture; it is hard to believe that these were actually worn when dancing. These dynamic sculptures, goddesses of the earth and of female fertility, require open space to assert themselves fully. Essentially solar and beneficent, they dominate Baga art and embody power through form.

The well-known large Banda masks are skilfully constructed and combine elements of the crocodile and the antelope with apparently human features. The Baga have few statuettes but numerous female puppets attached to sticks and carried during propitiatory ceremonies for the cultivation of rice.

Birds, which play an important role in the Baga pantheon, are used on the same occasions and testify to the inventiveness of the artist (page 138/1 and 2).

The Kissi and Mende have for centuries been carving statuettes in steatite (a soft stone often called soapstone) for funeral sites. Some of them, like the large head at the Museum of Primitive Art, New York (page 140/1), probably portray deceased ancestors while others, representing human figures bent over in attitudes of deep meditation (page 140/2), remind us of the Bakongo funeral statuettes; in fact, though their attitude is more lithe and almost oriental, the impression they make is very much the same. If we examine their faces only, we find that the shape and volume of their globular eyes remind us of the *Gelede** masks of the Yoruba and of the Dahomey Keitu area.

THE SIERRA LEONE MENDE MASKS

Of all Mende masks, the best known are the Bundu society helmets of darkened wood. These masks are very unusual in that they are worn by women.

The faces are adorned with an endless variety of hair-styles and we have never come across two identical specimens. Thus, even when the artist starts with a given, obligatory form, we find a strong tendency to improvise (page 143).

GURO. Mask in hardwood representing a human face with red and black patina. Monumental head-gear with refined and subtle decorations. Several such smiling masks — probably by the same sculptor — are known. Height: 35 cm.   Guro (Ivory Coast, central region).   Maurice Nicaud Collection, Paris.

THE SUDANESE REGION

In discussing the huge masks and statues of the Sudanese grasslands, it should be interesting to compare the ethnic groups of the Senufo (northern Ivory Coast area), the Bambara and Dogon, and the Kurumba, Mossi, Marka, Bobo and Lobi.

The art of these regions has many stylistic similarities, both in form and in spirit; the same synthesis of human and animal forms, the same elongated bodies, the same motif of horns decorating the masks. The Senufo occupy the north-west area of the Ivory Coast, and the various sub-styles radiate around Korhogo, the most characteristic centre with regard to sculpture. Here, as in many other parts of Africa, the sculptor, who is also a smith, belongs to a special caste. His art is secret and closely linked to the Poro initiation society rituals.

It is believed that the large pole-shaped sculptures were kept in a sacred wood, away from the sight of the uninitiated.

The specimen which we reproduce on page 23 is typical of the *Deble*. It is difficult to avoid a comparison with Egyptian art, especially as many of these statues (including one at the New York Museum of Primitive Art (page 21) and another at the Abidjan Museum) have an openwork disc above their head; these discs are undoubtedly symbols of the sun.

In any case, these are absorbed, ' inward ' forms as opposed to the forms of naturalistic sculpture. (As Rodin said to his pupils, Maillol and Despiau: ' Form must burst forth from the centre and radiate. ')

Among the most amazing Senufo masks is the well-known ' fire-spitter ', a sort of horned hyena with open jaws, worn horizontally by the dancer. Some of these masks are Janus-faced and thus become real spatial compositions without any single preferential angle from which they are to be viewed.

The most classical of the Senufo masks — one which has been frequently copied and has become a traditional figure — is endowed in its original version with both majesty and power as a result of the strict perfection of its proportions (page 144/3). The creature represented by this mask is symbolically linked to the earth by two tiny legs. This is a rare device in African art. The bird is an important symbol among the Senufo: whether gigantic or small, it protects the hut and the village, appearing frequently on masks and on nearly all the classical bas-reliefs which adorn the doors of dwellings or granaries.

AGNI. Fertility statuette in hardwood with light transparent patina and natural hair. Scarifications on face, neck and back. Like the Baule, the Agni brides received these beneficent statuettes which were kept in the married couple's home. In this example, of great sensibility, the artist has carried refinement so far as to hammer out the eye globes to give them expression.

Height: 42.5 cm.   *Agni (Ivory Coast, western region).*   *H. Duperrier Collection, Paris.*

The chameleon, symbol of longevity, even of eternity, is present on many sculptures. Further to the north, the Bambara, whose large wooden figures, male and female, call to mind the Senufo *Deble*, have a great variety of masks, ceremonial figures, puppets and ritual implements. An extensive study would be required to survey all the plastic variations on the antelope theme. These tall shapes, which fit on the dancers' heads by means of a small inverted basket, represent either the male animal or the female with its little one on its back (page 25). These masks are worn during the ritual agricultural dances which take place at sowing time and which appeal for good crops: *Chi wara* is the symbol of agriculture.

Broadly speaking, there are two tendencies among this abundance of forms: a tendency towards the horizontal (probably the older) and a tendency towards the vertical; the latter is often more abstract and allows the artist greater freedom to exercise his imagination.

In addition to ritual significance, these works seem to have an element of pure creativity, they seem to be a sort of stylistic exercise comparable to a Bach variation. One begins to dream — no doubt, aesthetically, a very Western dream — of the possibility of comparing the finest and most unusual *Chi wara* known (page 148/1).

We cannot study the Bambara facial masks without referring to the authoritative work of Professor Zaban who has described them and attributed them to the great *N'Domo** and *Kore** societies. The N'Domo masks have human features and are covered with cowrie shells; they are surmounted by between five and eight fingers, each number having a particular meaning. The Kore masks represent lions or hyenas, very abstract but recognisable. During dancing, these two masks confront each other.

The large Buguni ' queens ' (page 29) are of recent discovery, which does not mean that they are modern. On the contrary, the erosion of the wood and the purity of their archaic shape endow them with an architectural power and a kind of remoteness difficult to attribute to a particular period. Horsemen, carved in heavy darkened wood, are less frequent. The horseman is a theme common to both the Bambara and the Dogon.

The large Dogon horseman which we reproduce on page 33 is undoubtedly one of the finest African sculptures. Apart from any possible significance it may have, the triangulation of its forms, the tense energy and dignity of the man together with an exceptional uniformity of technique endow this sculpture with an intensity which places it among the undisputable masterpieces. For this is the conscious creation of a purposeful artist who triumphed over his material rather than merely adapting it to a conventional shape, as sometimes happens with Dogon sculptures. This conventionality, which gives us almost a kind of ' ready-made ' art, would

KRINJABO. Funeral terracotta representing the deceased. These sculptures were shaped and baked by women and placed on the porch-roof of cemeteries. Intact specimens such as this one are rare.
Height: 39 cm.   Krinjabo (Ivory Coast, region of Assini).   Musée des Arts Africains et Océaniens, Paris.

deserve a study extending to the entire continent, were it not for the fact that the word 'almost' implies that each African area has its own style and individual trademark.

The origin of the *tellem** is still a mystery: the wooden relics of this 'pre-style' are covered with a thick layer — probably of blood — and their long sojourn in grottos has made them mouldy.

The art which seems to proceed from these early quests for form does not in any way break the continuity of the quests, nor does it lack interest. Perhaps it is an attempt to achieve greater power by means of deliberately balanced structures (like the seated couples), of 'Cubist' planes and volumes which depend on one another and which are related to the form — nearly always tubular — of the torso. The masks are pure syntheses of animal forms — the cynocephalus, the hare — and all have clearly defined functions which Marcel Griaule has discussed in detail.

The so-called 'multi-tiered' masks, sometimes as much as five metres (about 16 feet) in height, and *kanaga** masks, shaped like the cross of Lorraine, were and are carried during funeral ceremonies.

For the Dogon, each carved or painted symbol has a precise significance recognised by all. Even the doors of granaries have their symbols — which serve to protect, to represent, and to communicate. These doors (like the one reproduced on page 35) are usually small and covered with carved animals or with crowds of people begging for rain; carved in parallel rows and repeated obsessively, they give the impression of a chorus of cries resounding on a wave-length imperceptible to us.

The 'ritual' object at New York's Museum of Primitive Art (page 151) represents the eight original ancestors of humanity holding up the world: this should prove that the Dogon saw the world in the shape of a globe. Though rather small, this extraordinary sculpture seems to have no physical scale: even if it were huge, it would lose nothing of its beauty and deep significance.

Here we are inclined to deplore the fact that the Africans lacked the technical means to create monumental works.

Both the Bambara and the Dogon embody the theme of fertility either in figures of hermaphrodites — symbols of complementary forms of creativity — or in representations of motherhood, which are among the most fundamentally African of such works. It is probable that in

ASHANTI. Funeral head in terracotta. These heads are believed to have been made about one hundred and fifty years ago by the Kwahu, an Ashanti group which at that time lived in what is now the Ewe country. Usually, sculptures of this type have round, flat faces set at a marked angle in relation to the neck. This example, however, relies on thickness and volume for its effect.

Height: 24 cm.   *Ashanti (Republic of Ghana, southern region).*   *British Museum, London.*

79

many other ethnic groups the mother-and-child theme is derived from Western influences and does not adapt itself well to a system of thought which is seldom representative and very rarely explanatory. This is one of the big differences between Negro art and Romanesque art, with its direct allusions.

The seated statue (page 31) with its light-red patina is rigid in shape: a slight vibration of lines gives it a human touch which contrasts with the stony face of the mother and the hardness of line of the child; yet, the work emanates a sort of tenderness — although one hesitates to use this word before so much apparent indifference — which makes of it a kind of archetype of the perpetuation of life. Another statue (page 37), sombre in spirit and of a dark material, even more archaic and austere, is no less beautiful and impressive.

The sculpture of the Kurumba, related to the Bambara, is very original and has become well known; many recent discoveries are considered fairly modern. The example reproduced on page 41 and belonging to the Faculty of Letters, Strasbourg, is authentic and was worn during ritual dances; like the Bambara *Chi wara*, it has its pair, and together they form a couple. This tribe has also produced a sort of helmet topped with a small, hollowed-out plank, resembling certain motifs of the neighbouring Mossi.

The Mossi have created few anthropomorphic sculptures, since the influence of Islam was strongly felt. There are only certain masks representing female figures with protruding chests which have a powerful simplicity of line. Other masks are topped with planks measuring as much as two metres, reminiscent of the multi-tiered Dogon masks. The few Mossi statuettes we know of have probably been removed from broken masks.

Marka art is closely linked to Bambara art. It cannot be called a sub-style, for most of its productions are truly masterly. Its themes remind us of the armour, knights and secret societies of the European Middle Ages; there is precision and austere power under the exquisitely decorated metal plating. Usually the masks are made of heavy hardwood (page 47).

The varied and colourful sculptures of the Bobo represent mother earth as a source of nourishment. They are round-faced masks (page 158/1) with a beak which curves downwards to meet the mouth; above, they are adorned with symbolically decorated planks, mostly painted in white, black and red, but sometimes also in blue.

In certain instances, a single object may combine details of both water and earth creatures: human features may be joined to the fins and tail of fish or the striped ears and horns of hinds or gazelles (pages 43 and 157). Mossi abstraction and Bambara realism — both powerful and dynamic styles — are combined in Bobo art, which is full of movement and designed for the use of dancers.

YORUBA. Brightly painted mask in light wood, for the ' Gelede' cult. These masks are always worn in pairs. The shape surmounting the head like a tiara is the stylisation of a kerchief in beautifully blended colours. Height: 21 cm.   Yoruba-Keitu (east of the Dahomey Republic).   Descazeaux Collection, Paris.

The Lobi are sometimes considered the 'poor relations' of African art. However, if we examine the human head reproduced on page 49, we must disagree with this too-hasty judgement. The treatment of volumes, and their interplay, the abstract austerity of expression not unlike that of Chinese art of the Golden Age, make us feel that we are in the presence of African art at its best. Most Lobi statues and statuettes are of more primitive make: they are carved straight out of the wood, often taking advantage of the shape of the trunk (page 159) or branch; the heads are roughened down rather than carved, but this very hardness gives them power. Some of the figures are dual — embodying both the male and the female principle — and represent in all likelihood the human being prior to circumcision and initiation. There is little or no brass casting, and the gold-weights ascribed to the Lobi come either from the Senufo — excellent founders — or from the Baule, further south.

THE DAN OR YAKUBA

In his remarkable study on the frontier between the Ivory Coast and Liberia, Jean Girard casts light on the problem raised by the famous Dan, Ngere, Wobe, Guerze, Kran and Kru masks which have long been admired by connoisseurs.

Girard starts off by specifying that there is no Dan style — the word draws its origin from the city of Danane. The style is actually that of the Yakuba.

NOK. Terracotta head in coarse clay mixed with mica. The face is carved in a strict cylinder as we can see from the profile and the front. It was found by Bernard Fagg in 1943 during the Nok excavations. Circa 500-200 BC.

Height: 23 cm.   Nok Civilisation (Nigerian Federal Republic, central region).   Nigerian Museums.

The beautiful masks, three specimens of which are reproduced on pages 51, 53 and 161/3, are too well known to require description; they are used in dancing and are called *Tehegla**.

Masks of the same style but with wide-open, round eyes (page 161/4) serve quite another purpose. As symbols of virility, they are used once a year during a sort of inter-village race in the course of which the mask-carriers chase other young men, thus commemorating the mythical event when masked men took hold of women for the first time. Girard mentions further that, contrary to a generally accepted opinion, these very refined and polished masks do not represent specifically female features but merely the quality of beauty (masculine beauty is very important in Negro Africa, and no equivocal meaning is attached to it). Girard counted up as many as seventeen types of masks along with their specific functions; the fine specimen reproduced on page 57 is surrounded with bells and called *Gla**. Another well-known specimen with a human face ending up in a bird's beak (toucan or hornbill) is called *Koposry* and presides over ploughing, sowing and harvesting. The tubular-eyed *Koma*, which Picasso admits having used in some of his collages and paintings, takes precedence over all other masks in the area. Its role, among others, is to baffle the sorcerers and counteract their spells, to discover and enforce observance of truth, in other words, to act as a supreme supernatural umpire. The secret Yakuba societies — Ngere-Wobe — have small 'pocket-masks' made either in bronze (very rare) or, much more frequently, in darkened polished wood. They indicate the rank conferred by the above-mentioned societies on their carriers.

Sculpture as such is rather poor, except for a few works representing mother and child (page 55). Much more primitive than the Baule versions of this subject — all of which are of recent origin — the broken style of these masks, which are sometimes as large as the body itself, gives them a powerful, stocky stability.

BAULE

It is well known that the Baule come from the Ashanti kingdom; at the beginning of the eighteenth century they emigrated to the middle of the present Ivory Coast where they settled down. They brought with them their traditions and techniques — mainly brass- and gold-casting — which they still maintain. Baule art, as famous in Africa and elsewhere as Romanesque art in Europe, calls to mind both the wise, pensive ancestral figures and the finely polished masks with their transparent patina and their delicate decorations made up of plaits, horns and pecking birds.

To the Western eye this art is like an open door, and even if its mystery and significance lie

NOK. Terracotta head in coarse clay mixed with mica. Like the preceding one, it was discovered by Bernard Fagg in 1943 in the course of the Nok excavations. Same estimated date. Height: 22.9 cm.   Nok Civilisation (Nigerian Federal Republic, central region).   Nigerian Museums.

elsewhere and may remain secret, we, who are fed on Egyptian and Greek civilisation and on Romanesque and Gothic art, are immediately drawn by its magic spell.

Thus, it is thanks to the Baule that many art-lovers have learned to appreciate African art, even though — be it said to their credit — they have soon extended their vision and knowledge to styles which, at first sight, may have bewildered them. What accounts for this immediate response is the fact that these sculptures are almost always benevolent and, one feels, protective. Neither must we overlook the love of the Baule themselves for the best of their creations, if we can judge by the wonderful patina they were able to obtain through infinite patience and care; this very dedication and love is, to a large extent, communicated to those who contemplate these masterpieces.

The mask surmounted by a bird, probably a toucan (page 67), is a striking example. Another mask representing an ancestor (page 61), full of dignity and wisdom and as if illumined from within, is surmounted by three fingers, bent forward. Apart from its exceptional beauty, we think that it is one of the most ancient specimens known, and its perfect state of preservation proves the care with which it has been protected against the injuries of time. It is impossible, of course, to determine when it was made.

The large ancestral figure reproduced on page 63 is undoubtedly one of the most important sculptures in Africa and of an unusual realism. The beard, the hair-style — everything contributes to the life-like effect; it is a portrait, no longer an archetype. It would be interesting to

IFE. Portrait of an Oni, or king. Thin bronze, uniform casting, lost-wax technique. Parallel scarifications over the entire face. Shiny green patina. Found in 1938-39 during excavations in the vicinity of the Oni's palace at Ife, together with seventeen other bronzes. The mongol features stressed by William Fagg, with a nose more aquiline than negroid, can be explained by the presence of Hamitic races, such as the Fulani in West-Africa. Height: 31 cm.   Ancient Ife (Nigerian Federal Republic, central region).   Ife Museum.

86

87

consider of some of these African statues whether they are intended as representational portraits of their own race, as abstract types not based on any model, or as composites of several models ?

We cannot help feeling that some of the masks and statuettes born of the plastic inventiveness of this continent remind us fleetingly of certain faces and attitudes. However, the very power of this art prevents us from placing our recollection. We are not here referring to royal portraits, which are rare; the likeness of these to the real models has never been established.

Everything leads us to believe that the African sculptor tends to represent the idea rather than the shape of the human being, and that fundamental details such as heads, hands and sexual features merely define its function. Among the Ivory Coast population, the so-called fecundity statuettes play a specific social role: they are offered to the bride by her parents-in-law who hope for numerous grandchildren. Its glossy orange patina has given the appearance of old ivory to the wooden statue reproduced on page 75; this patina suggests that the statuette has been frequently appealed to by women hoping for children.

Like their neighbours in the Senufo area, many of the doors of Baule huts are decorated with various motifs: caymans and fish devouring each other, snakes, tortoises, masks and even — perhaps under Sudanese influence — horsemen and horses, ox-pecker birds and crocodiles. Many of these doors are of masterly composition and, once again, reminiscent of Egypt (page 59). Unfortunately they are exposed to torrential rains and changes of temperature, and it is therefore unlikely that ancient examples could have survived; those which are still to be seen are merely replicas of the past.

GURO — YAURE

The Guro are neighbours of the Baule to the north-west; their masks, though very similar in shape and structure to those of the Baule, are more extensively decorated. High headdresses and plaits lengthen the sculpture, giving it greater height (page 71). Usually the wood is finished with a light, transparent, yet deep red colour. This varnish is obtained by crushing certain seeds which contain a powerful dye and probably mixing them with local oils; the varnish penetrates the wood and gives it the gloss and hardness of lacquer (page 73).

The Guro masks are frequently without nostrils, the mouth half-opened in a sort of smile. Except for the small gold-weights decorated with seemingly joyful animals, there are few smiling masks in Africa. The Yaure are situated between the Guro and the Baule; their style has been

IFE. Fragment of terracotta head. Very probably the portrait or representation of an Oni, similar to the bronze heads of the same style and characteristics. It is assumed that these moulds, eventually baked, were used as preliminary studies for eventual casting in metal. This is the first example of its kind found by Western research workers. The British Museum has a mould attributed to the beginning of this century.
Height: 13 cm.   Ancient Ife (Nigerian Federal Republic, central region).   Guennol Collection, New York.

influenced by both neighbours. The faces are usually surrounded by a zig-zag frame and possibly topped with one or two birds. The example which we have chosen (page 169) is well known. Published in 1927, it belonged to the Paul Guillaume Collection and has only recently been bought by the Musée des Arts Africains et Océaniens, Paris. Actually, there used to be a second bird matching the one overhanging the face. Unfortunately, it broke off and was lost. Another, very similar mask, belonging to the Royal Museum of Scotland, Edinburgh, still has the two toucans pecking in the central cup.

Except for a few pieces of minor importance, the Yaure and Guro have produced no statuettes.

Although we are here concerned with African sculpture, masks and figures, rather than with domestic, utilitarian and magical implements, it is difficult, when referring to the three ethnic groups under consideration, to disregard the innumerable loom pulleys, real works of art despite their necessarily small size. They can be considered a domestic counterpart of the large carvings, a daily and permanent token of its existence.

AGNI

The Agni who originated in the Assinian area east of the Great Bassam are known mainly for their terracotta figures, made by people of the old Krinjabo kingdom. These figures, which are a schematic representation of the dead, were probably the work of women. Unlike some older

IFE. Torso of a king. Bronze with shiny green patina. Here the coral necklaces and chains worn by kings are painted in red. This is the upper part of an upright statue. We know of another example which is complete. The one we reproduce, probably broken because of the frailty of the bronze, still has its internal core in blackened earth. Classical period between the twelfth and fourteenth centuries. Found at Wunmonije.

90   *Height: 37 cm.*   *Ancient Ife (Nigerian Federal Republic, central region).*   *Ife Museum.*

relics (especially the Nok heads), these terracottas were baked in embers, in a temperature probably too low to ensure fusion. One of these heads, accidentally broken, revealed fragments of human or animal matter very much resembling a part of the brain; from this it may be deduced that the object was a reliquary. Some of these figures were of great stylistic purity, but the majority have been broken and reduced to fragments.

ASHANTI

We know that in the seventeenth and even eighteenth centuries the social structure of the Ashanti was almost feudal. Their country was one of the gold trading centres where the goldsmith's craft was highly developed. Unfortunately, little has remained of this past achievement, mercenary considerations having prevailed over artistic values, and most of these objects having been sold or melted down. In England, we can still admire the famous mask owned by the Wallace Collection and the large decorative insignia, of more recent origin, in the British Museum: such insignia were worn by chiefs and kings during ceremonies. The Baule continued the practice of wearing similar insignia, and until quite recently they decorated their velvet caps with similar but smaller ones.

The Ashanti, known for their metal craft in bronze and brass, have some wonderfully-cast receptacles called *kuduo**; these have lids featuring animal fights and scenes similar to those decorating the proverb-weights. The *kuduo* reproduced on page 172/3 represents a king surrounded by his musicians.

The dolls with large discoidal heads (page 172/2) called *Akua ba*, are beneficent fecundity figures carried by pregnant women to ensure the birth of healthy and well-formed children. The same type of face inside an almost perfect circle decorates pottery of various sizes, terracotta objects, and combs made of hardwood. As for the brass gold-weights, which are not included in our survey, there is an infinite variety of them and the Ashanti may rightly claim to have been their originators.

No specific style can be claimed for the Togo sculptures; the famous buffalo head at the New York Museum of Primitive Art is unfortunately one of the very few examples to have survived (page 174/1). The rhythmic interplay of curves and planes and the masterly technique whereby hardened and polished terracotta acquires the appearance of bronze make us think regretfully of all the works irremediably lost.

In the history of African art, the Dahomey are known chiefly for their so-called court art. In addition, however, they have produced the famous ' war gods ', unusual improvisations

IFE. Head of an Oni. Bronze with a dark brown-green patina spotted with red. The holes surrounding the forehead, cheeks and lips were used to fix the hair and beard. Masterpiece of the classical period.

Height: 29 cm.   Ancient Ife (Nigerian Federal Republic, central region).   Nigerian Museums.

revealing a sense of humour and an unconventional inventiveness which we hope to see in future works.

Apart from the famous clay bas-reliefs which decorate the palace walls and which have been so often remodelled and repainted as to have become depressingly sugary, Dahomey craftsmanship includes realistic wooden animals with embossed plating. It is difficult to speak about more recent works, whether of wood or of metal; the unrestrained claims of commercialism have weakened and nearly crippled all original creative power, reducing the artist to the anonymous production of standardised if exotic objects.

Near the western frontier bordering on Nigeria, the *Gelede* masks which are found around Keitu actually belong to the Yoruba cycle. Most of the sculptures of the Nago tribe are primitive and anecdotal. However, in the presence of the pure and masterfully constructed mask reproduced on page 81, we should refrain from too rash a judgement, for here again the influence of Egypt is apparent.

NOK — IFE — MIDDLE AND LOWER NIGER

We know of Bernard Fagg's wonderful discovery of the Nok civilisation. This discovery is all the more important since, apart from the plastic quality of this art, it dates from the last centuries BC and is thus the oldest sculpture in Negro Africa.

Austere and powerful, with pronounced features and bare volumes — cylindrical or symmetrically stylised heads (pages 83 and 177), this style calls to mind that of some Mediterranean

IFE. Terracotta head. Face scarified with parallel grooving and surmounted by a royal crown. The modelling is of great precision, like that of a bronze. Probably represents one of the first Onis.
Height: 16 cm.   Ancient Ife (Nigerian Federal Republic, central region).   Nigerian Museums.

civilisations, though retaining its typical and even enigmatic features. Only heads without bodies have reached us. From the way they have been broken, we can infer that the firing technique was defective: probably not all Africans had discovered pottery furnaces and many of them, including the Agni, Krinjabo, and Ivory Coast Ashanti, used embers from a hot but open-air fire, obviously resulting in a dispersion of heat. At Katiola (Baule area) and in many other places in Africa, the same method is still used for the firing of domestic jars.

When studying the relics of Nok art, it is difficult to associate it with its closest relative in the area, the Ife art. As William Fagg points out: 'Unless Nok civilisation has lasted much longer than we have reason to believe, we are faced with an historical gap of a thousand years or more, which leaves us free to speculate as to the possible relationship between Nok civilisation and humanistic Ife art. This phenomenon presents the biggest problem in all the history of the art of Negro Africa.' Perhaps this problem will eventually be solved; nonetheless let us remember that, as Valery had said, 'civilisations are mortal' — a statement that history has proved over and over again to be true.

Amidst the great variety of African art, sometimes crude, sometimes delicate, sometimes boisterous and violent, Ife art is like an oasis of peace, both for the mind and for the eye.

This quality may separate it from other styles of African sculpture, but such a form of expression has nevertheless a greater appeal for people of other continents and is more universally understood.

The famous terracottas (already known to Leo Frobenius who had them carefully cast) have elsewhere been thoroughly described. Likewise, the eighteen magnificent twelfth- and thirteenth-century bronzes discovered later are well known and their possible resemblance to Egyptian art has been much discussed. It is quite gratuitous to point to such a resemblance, however, especially if we consider that, at the same time, stone cutters in southern France, at Souillac and Moissac, influenced by Byzantium, were carving prophets with elongated faces bearing more resemblance to the Nok faces than the bronzes under consideration. Only the perfection of the *cire perdue* technique may reveal an Egyptian influence in the technical organisation of the casting shop. What is certain is that this was the only area which produced large-size bronzes such as the famous cross-legged statue of the isle of Tada and the Jebba archer (page 180/1 and jacket).

The large heads, presumably portraying deceased kings, are usually lifesize. The holes delimiting the areas of hair and beard were probably used to fix bead ornaments or real hair.

Although all these admirable statues are linked by a common style, the artists who carved them

BENIN. Upright figure with raised arms. Bronze cast in the lost-wax technique and with a dark brown patina. Very rare example of Benin female statuette. The decoration on the base — a bow and arrow — suggests that this figure is a patroness of the hunt. In any case, one of the enigmatic masterpieces of this style.

Height: 46 cm.   *Benin (Nigerian Federal Republic).*   *Museum of Ethnography, Berlin-Dahlem.*

97

were obviously very differently inspired. The head reproduced on page 179 is actually a mask: the slits under the eyes allow for vision. The precision of the planes, the deliberate simplification of forms reduced to the essential for all their plenitude, together give the impression of a work cut directly from hard basalt rather than modelled in clay or wax. The terracottas of the same origin are usually smaller and, although the corresponding bronzes have not been found, one may assume that they were preliminary studies for future moulds. This, however, is merely an hypothesis.

Though less concise in style, certain fragments emanate so much intensity and radiance as to achieve the level of genuine masterpieces (pages 89 and 95).

What William Fagg calls the art of Middle and Lower Niger can apparently be situated in time between the Ife civilisation and the beginnings of the important Benin industry.

The marvellous statuette of the returning huntsman, now in the British Museum (page 105), is an amazing work of art, almost transcending questions of style: the artist, though obviously attempting realism, based his composition on squares, one rectangle being formed by the legs and another by the torso and arms, the whole statue acquiring thereby a strength and stability which neither the fluidity of lines nor the richness of decoration can impair.

BENIN

About the fifteenth century, the Bini, inheritors of Ife tradition and technique, began to produce all kinds of sculptures and reliefs, mostly for royal palaces. Many travellers who visited the area tell of their amazement when they discovered the walls and doors of princely dwellings covered with richly decorated brass plates. The figures stand out in relief against a background embossed with floral ornaments.

William Fagg has made a thorough study of the bronzes of this particular style and has been able to date them with precision. As a result, we are able to trace the development of this style from its beginnings, when it was still dependent on the past, to its period of consolidation and, finally, to the weakening of its forms and the deterioration of its technique in the eighteenth and especially the nineteenth centuries. The present replicas, cast and sold on the spot to tourists at an almost officially established price, are of inferior quality. The metal is poor and incapable of acquiring a fine patina; the objects lack style and have become mere caricatures of ancient models.

BENIN. Bronze horseman of the intermediate period, second half of the seventeenth century. The head-gear is similar to that worn by the bodyguards of certain chiefs in present-day Northern Nigeria. The figure probably represents a visiting emissary to the court of Benin. The interlacing on the base is reminiscent of certain decorative motifs of the Bakuba.
Height: 59.3 cm.   *Benin (Nigerian Federal Republic).*   *British Museum, London.*

We find yet another reminder of Egypt in the hair-style of the oldest brass heads. It is only later, towards the beginning of the sixteenth century, that the remarkable heads of queen-mothers appear. Of these, only a few specimens are known: at the British Museum, at Liverpool, one in Berlin and another belonging to the Nigerian Museums. Although they were supposed to portray the mothers of the then reigning Obas, we cannot fail to see that they are all alike and very young — mere girls, in fact. This makes us think that rather than representing the queen-mothers, they may have reproduced the features of the models.

Another type of face which appeared about the middle of the sixteenth century was produced until the middle of the nineteenth century: it is a large head, clamped into a cylinder representing superimposed coral necklaces (page 180/2). The brass, much thicker than that of the Ife heads or even of the early Benin heads, gives an impression of heaviness. This heaviness was probably necessary to stabilise the base and thus prevent the carved — and interchangeable — long ivory tusk embedded in the top of the crown from swaying. Similar wooden carvings of a much rougher make were probably designed for notables, bronze being reserved for the royal court.

One of the most unusual and at the same time beautiful examples of Benin art is undoubtedly the upright female figure with arms outstretched in blessing (page 97). It suggests a Hindu goddess or a Carolingian reliquary, but certainly not a West African statue ! One is fascinated by the enigmatic and impenetrable face, by the powerful simplicity of the body, with its two legs fitted like columns to the base of the torso. The only life-like elements are the arms and hands. Could it represent an African Diana (symbol on the pedestal) ?

Another very rare female figure in this style is the plaque representing a young girl carrying an aquamanile in the form of a leopard — a princely or royal emblem — on her left shoulder (page 178/3). The delicacy of the model, the sensitivity of the carving make this a real jewel of Benin art.

Among the numerous plaques at the British Museum, that of the drummer deserves special mention. Though not classical in composition, it has an unusual dynamism, and is almost musical in its movement and rhythm. The artist must have been exceedingly gifted; although his style is formal, his work conveys a sense of life. Benin plaques should be studied and illustrated as thoroughly as Romanesque capitals. Even though starting from quite different premises, they, too, have a didactic element. What a wonderful tale they tell and with what intensity ! They are like a precious manuscript on Africa. Many plaques have been lost, of course, but what art can hope to be preserved forever ?

BENIN. Bronze plaque with dark brown-green patina. Originally these plaques covered the poles of porches of the palace in Benin City. This specimen represents a drummer attached to the royal service, beating hollow wooden gongs.

Height: 45 cm.   *Benin (Nigerian Federal Republic).*   *British Museum, London.*

YORUBA

Carved from the very tip of the tusk, the wonderful horseman reproduced on page 176/1 (which can now be seen at the British Museum together with its double made by the same artist) is undeniably one of the most abstract and powerful works — regardless of size — of the whole of Yoruba art; nor can we remain indifferent to the acid charm of its purplish colour, the 'recipe' of which is unknown to us. Here again, the severity proceeds from the limitations of the material: wood and ivory impose a form which, though limited in size, proceeds from the material itself.

We should remember that the Yoruba kingdom is one of the largest in western Africa. Its population is estimated at five million, while geographically it projects beyond Nigeria, encroaches on Dahomey and Togo and extends as far as the Gold Coast.

Though lacking stylistic unity, the Yoruba share the same religious beliefs and worship more or less the same gods.

The artistic range of the Yoruba, from highly spiritualised forms (such as the *oshe-shango* in ivory or polished wood and certain masks with strict lines showing up the different planes) to the popular rustic groups, is a reflection of the range of life itself, comparable perhaps to the Middle Ages with their sanctuaries, altars and taverns.

AFO

The Afo, who live more or less in the centre of Nigeria, have produced some very impressive fertility statuettes; carved in parallel planes, they give the impression of being hurled into space. The famous mother-and-child in the Horniman Museum, London, illustrates these characteristics (page 185).

EKOI

The Ekoi, who live near the Cross River, produce amazing sculptures with human features. These are cap-masks in the form of articulated statuettes, large double helmet-masks, and faces topped with huge spiral-shaped horns entirely sheathed in antelope skin stretched to fit the shape of the wood. Though of a realism which is sometimes almost embarrassing, some of them are very beautiful (page 188/2).

BENIN. Upright figure in bronze with a shiny brown patina. Intermediate period. Probably represents a royal messenger, as he wears a Maltese cross on his chest. The loincloth is decorated with the small heads of Portuguese soldiers, identical with those that can be seen on certain bronze plaques of the same period. Height: 63.5 cm.   *Benin (Nigerian Federal Republic).*   *British Museum, London.*

IBIBIO

The Ibibio masks of the Ekkpe society are very expressive: usually blackened, with pronounced modulations of volume, they are sometimes reminiscent of the Ivory Coast Ngere-Wobe masks. The lower jaw is often movable. However, the example reproduced on page 184/1 is of a different style; used during ritual ceremonies of the above-mentioned society, it is much more naturalistic. The face has an expression of great spirituality and supreme detachment.

The elongated Ekpu statues (page 188/1) are of ancestral figures, probably of the Oron, one of the Ibibio clans. Thousands of these are known, many of them — according to William Fagg — dating from the seventeenth century. It is obvious that the artist was limited by the diameter of the wood and confined himself to giving it the desired shape. The technique and even the spirit of these statues call to mind the large monoliths recently discovered near Ikom (page 184/3). The latter, probably representing tribal chiefs, are carved or rather engraved in very hard basalt. The heads are an integral part of the total volume and are defined only by a slight modulation. The importance given to the navel may have a meaning which escapes us. The Nigerian Department of Antiquities has recorded about three hundred of these monoliths which open a new window on to African sculpture. Though it is still difficult to date them precisely, they were almost certainly made before the nineteenth century.

SAO — CAMEROONS

It is J.-P. Lebeuf who virtually discovered the strikingly expressive terracottas produced by the Sao culture; these representations of ancestors (page 189) have been attributed to the period between the tenth and sixteenth centuries.

The modelling is extremely realistic and refined, typical of the Fort-Foureau area, north of the Cameroons. The grooved face reproduced on page 107 is probably the fragment of a statuette. However, it seems to come from the same ancient empire that produced so many bronze works — ceremonial rings, cups cast in the *cire perdue* technique — all of which testify to great technical skill.

The Duala area surrounding the town has produced only one type of mask and very few if any statuettes. The masks, usually coloured, are geometric in style, and generally represent a slender bovid head. They are no longer to be found on the spot, and it is in Stuttgart, in the Linden-Museum, that the best examples can be admired.

BENIN. Represents the return from an antelope hunt. Bronze with dark green-brown patina. The huntsman seems overwhelmed by the weight of the animal he has killed. His dog is at his feet. Very free and imaginative work, quite different from the classical Benin statues ordered by the royal court.
Height: 36 cm.   Lower Niger bronze industry (Nigerian Federal Republic).   British Museum, London.

We must not overlook the unusual bow ornaments of racing canoes, still used today on important political or tribal occasions. These refined sculptures call Indonesian art to mind and lack the usual rigour of African sculpture. This, however, is neither the first nor the last example of baroque tendencies in Africa: though trying to shake off the idea of unity, it is unable to destroy it altogether. The famous Bamileke are known for their architecture, among the most striking in Africa.

They skilfully relate sculpture and structure: poles, door and window frames are no longer accessories but contribute to an overall impression of loftiness. Some of the chiefs' cabins measure as much as twenty metres. Raymond Lecocq has published an important study on this race of builders and sculptors. Present-day craftsmanship has become commercialised and the Bamileke 'panels' are produced merely for tourists, lacking in inspiration and of poor quality.

The large ceremonial bead-covered seats (page 193) representing fantastic surrealistic creatures from another world are rich and colourful relics of the past. We think this is one of the most impressive fusions of shape and colour.

Recent Bamileke sculpture is almost unique in expressing movement: we refer to the 'winding' mother-and-child figures, built in spirals and suggesting released springs.

The female figure of red wood at the Berlin-Dahlem Museum represents an ancestral figure, absorbed and tense (page 191). Statues of this type were set out in great numbers under the front porch of large houses.

Relics of refined ivory craftsmanship subsist to this day among the Bandjun and the Bagam. Many talented sculptors have devised characteristic faces, flat and grimacing.

The Bamum have been and still are producing many sculptures in hardwood and softwood (seats and masks), as well as skilfully chiselled ivory and metal works.

Sculpture adds ornamental and symbolic richness to the chief's dwellings. The round seats and rectangular beds are carved in openwork; the supporting elements are in the shape of animals — leopards and buffalo heads. The human masks are of a chubby type and only a few examples of the original style still exist.

Fortunately, one of the last Funban sultans understood the necessity of protecting ancient relics: he set up a museum attached to his palace where fine sculptures of this style are still kept. Metalcraft is mostly represented by ultra-ornate, sometimes monumental, pipes. Some faces still reveal Yoruba influence, while small masks, in bronze or brass, over-decorated and baroque, are the poor relatives of late Benin craftsmanship.

SAO. Small head in red terracotta. The scarification is concentric around the eyes, and in chevron pattern on the lower part of the face. Fragment of anthropomorphous statuette found in the ruins near Fort-Foureau. Height: 6.5 cm.   Sao (Cameroon Federal Republic).   Lafaille Natural History Museum, La Rochelle.

FANG

Buried in the heart of one of the thickest and dampest forest in West Africa, the Fang tribe, which is a large one, have been forced to become more or less wanderers by their need to find new land for cultivation. However, during the time we have been able to study their art, *i.e.* from the beginning of this century, they seem to have succeeded in maintaining their original style throughout their wanderings, carrying with them their strength, their faith and their secrets.

In discussing African art, many writers have tried to oppose the style of the grasslands to the style of the forests, contrasting the dynamism of the former with the introspection of the latter. Such a contrast may be tempting and even satisfying, but it may prove deceptive. There are immediate problems arising from such a theory: in the first place, how does Dogon art fit in? Fang art seduced artists and amateurs as soon as it became known in Europe, and it is still held in the greatest esteem despite other discoveries. In an increasingly limited and competitive market, the Pahuin statues are still sought after, both for their extreme rarity (Pierre Vérité states his amazement when he saw about eighty-four statues of this style collected in one place, whereas the Baule ancestral statues and the Ivory Coast masks of similar style can be counted by the thousands) and for their intrinsic quality. Their lofty harmony, their richness of form and vitality disdain undue decorations; these funerary representations seem to seek a convergence of life-before-birth and life-after-death. We know that these figures have traditionally ended up in a basket made of bark (called *bieri*) containing the bones of the dead as well as magic powders concealed in the horns of gazelles.

The fine example in the New York Museum of Primitive Art (page 198/1) is typical of this modulated and sustained style.

The British sculptor, Jacob Epstein, acquired many Fang statuettes and heads from Paul Guillaume, a judicious collector and merchant. Most of them are scattered, but fortunately the large flat face with the huge forehead, so often publicised, is now in New York and accessible to the public (Museum of Primitive Art).

Masks of this ethnic group are rare. Carved in soft bombax wood and whitewashed with kaolin, they have bulging foreheads and concave cheeks which end up in a point forming the mouth. It is believed that their ritual purpose — like that of so many African masks — is to detect sorcerers and to dispel fears and evil spells. It is clear that, with a few exceptions, African sculpture plays a protective and beneficent role.

BAMILEKE. *Mask representing the head of a buffalo. Wood covered with cylindrical beads of various colours fixed to a net closely fitting the shape of the mask. The carved and painted wood is revealed in the lower part of the horns.*
Height: 84 cm.   Bafret (Cameroon Federal Republic).   Treasury of the Bamileke Chiefs.

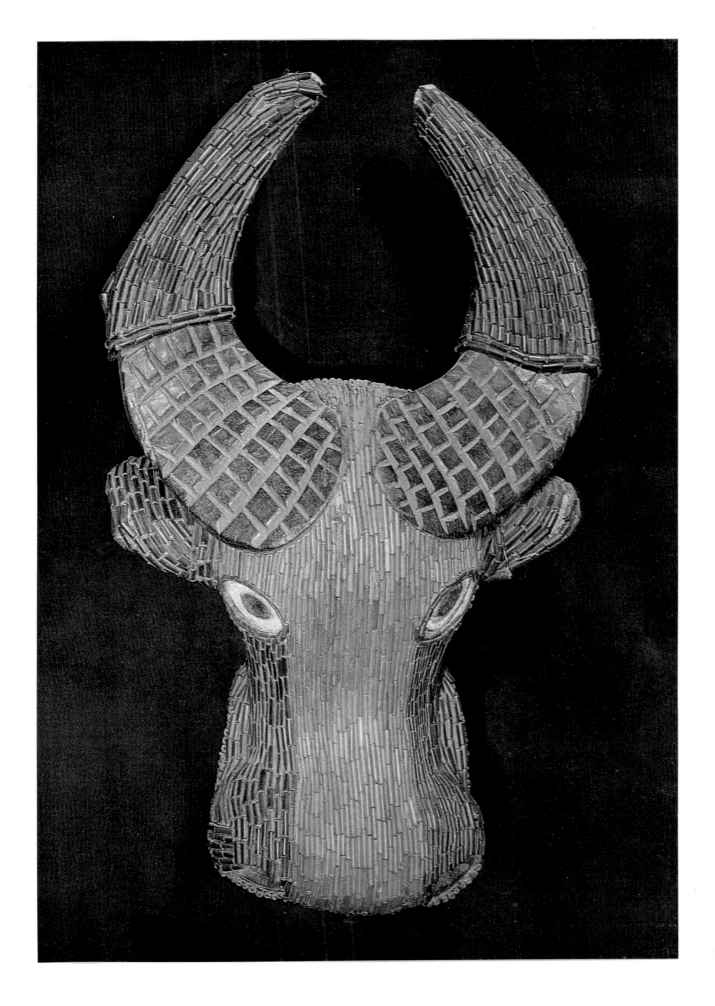

BAKOTA

The Bakota are neighbours of the Fang and have more or less the same funerary customs. They too keep the bones of their dead in plaited bark or rush receptacles, topped — like the Pahuin — with a figure representing the soul of the dead. Here, however, the resemblance ceases. There is a much freer use of form among the Bakota. When and by whom was created the prototype of these oval faces, convex or concave, sheathed in copper or brass, or with lamellae arranged in parallel or opposed rows? What is their meaning ? If we examine a group of them together we shall be even more disconcerted. Some of them radiate a sort of 'solar' power like pagan monstrances, while others, of a sinister and even dangerous aspect (but perhaps this is a subjective feeling), symbolise the fear of the unknown. In any case, every one of them stands out in its own right. The specimen reproduced on pages 114 and 115 is one of the rare double-faced examples: one of its faces is convex, the other concave. Philippe Guimiot, who has studied on the spot this particular ethnic group as well as the neighbouring groups, relates this sculpture to the dead-twin cult, a cult already practised in another form by the Yoruba, who reverently kept and fed two small statuettes. It would be interesting to learn what Bakota art looked like in its beginnings, before copper and brass were imported from Europe and used to cover the hulls of wooden ships to protect them from teredo worms below the waterline. However, we cannot hope to discover any such early objects, since the soft wood used in their manufacture could never have survived in these forests saturated with humidity night and day, with seldom a ray of sunshine.

In any case, even though we may never learn more about it, all these yellow stars, more or less brilliant or pale, will continue to cast their disquieting light.

The helmet-masks of the Bakota-Hongwe sub-tribe are impressively architectural in their interplay of volumes. When we look at the sculptures kept in the Musée des Arts Africains et Océaniens and examine them from every angle, we cannot help regretting that, with a few exceptions mostly influenced by Islam, Negro Africa has produced no purely Negro architecture of durable materials.

M'PONGWE — BAPUNU

When approaching Gaboon from the western coast, we come upon the M'Pongwe people, who were credited — wrongly — with the carving of very beautiful masks still bearing the name of this ethnic group (pages 117, 201 and 202/2). Actually, these masks were conceived

FANG. Head in wood with a dark patina; the eyes are suggested by a yellowish wax. Top of a reliquary called 'bieri', consisting of a bark basket in which the Fang kept the bones of ancestors mingled with magic substances.

110   *Height: 40 cm.*   *Fang-Pahuin (Gaboon Republic).*   *Henri Kamer Collection, Cannes.*

III

by the Bapunu, who lived in the hinterland. Their shape, reminiscent of Japanese art, the pureness and gracefulness of their execution which is yet not devoid of a certain mannerism in the less beautiful specimens, suggest foreign influence if not imitation. Africa has for centuries been subjected to varied influences, especially along the coast. (A reliable witness came across a Ming vase among the Dogon, some twenty years ago.) In any case, and even though we may never be able to find an explanation, Bapunu art, geographically so near the non-naturalistic Fang and the Mitsogo, raises fascinating problems as to its actual 'status'. The neighbouring Mitsogo have produced carved pillars which support the roofs of initiation huts; these pillars, of a refined and introspective style (page 203/4), are known in only very few examples.

BAKWELE

The Bakwele have been known and singled out for their concave, sometimes openwork, heart-shaped masks ever since the West became acquainted with Negro art. The example reproduced on page 204/1 belongs to the La Rochelle Museum and is one of the most powerfully conceived sculptures, projected as it were into space. Together with the Dogon *kanaga*, it is considered by André Malraux to be among the masterpieces of African art. The Bakwele have also produced flat masks, probably funeral masks, representing animal instead of human shapes. One of these is kept at the British Museum and is the abstract image of a koba antelope.

One technical element is common to all these types of 'flat' sculptures: the eye is always on the surface of the wood, and it is set off by a kind of hollow dug out around it. The same ethnic group has produced another type of mask which is totally different from the 'classical' ones: bulging, with very marked curves, the upper part is human while the lower part represents a boar's muzzle. Only very few examples have reached us. One of them was published in *Sculptures africaines et océaniennes* by Clouzot and Level, while another is kept in the Musée des Arts Africains et Océaniens (page 204/2).

BATEKE

In the Stanley Pool area, the Bateke have produced a large quantity of statuettes ranging in size from a few centimetres in height (the most numerous) to as much as fifty centimetres, although these are very rare (page 206/1). Spontaneous and rhythmic in style, they are considered, like the Oron ancestral statuettes, among the most hieratic of African sculpture. They are supposed to accompany the child to manhood, whereupon they become ineffective and expendable.

FANG. Head in light-coloured hardwood. The hieratically stylised face is whitewashed with kaolin. A hole is carved out in the back of the head to hold a stick or a stalk. Does not seem to have been used as a reliquary. Height: 30.5 cm.   Fang (Gaboon Republic).   Descazeaux Collection, Paris.

Let us quote A. Maesen:

' In contrast to the beliefs of most Africans, the Teke seem to believe that the spirits of ancestors have no direct influence over the destiny of their descendants. Their intervention, which is by no means underrated, operates through the medium of an unlimited number of supernatural forces (whether personalised or not, it is difficult to state). The protection of the young child, until the age of initiation, commonly attributed to these statuettes, reveals to us merely a fragment of a much wider and extremely complex civilisation.'

The Bateke masks, small abstract planks in which the human resemblance is reduced not to the essential but rather to the minimum — the face is no more than hinted at — pose a problem of authenticity: the beautiful and very much admired specimen in the Musée de l'Homme appears never to have been used. Others, no less remarkable as regards inventiveness, are disputed by experts. The fact that they bear little relation to the 'authentic' sculptures of this style brings no element of certainty. They must be taken for what they are — successful and original plastic works in their own right. The day is not far off when relatively modern African sculpture will have to be studied not with a view to 'desanctifying' it but to pointing out that even though it has long ceased to be a cult object, it has, apart from commercial craftsmanship, produced works worthy of interest. Always referring to the Bateke style, let us mention the chief's necklaces, exquisitely cast and incised in bronze or brass with simple and archaic geometrical motifs. They are certainly superb examples of the jewellery produced in this part of Africa.

BAKOTA. Large double reliquary figure with a concave face on one side and a convex face on the other. Wood plated with pale yellow brass. Used for the protection of reliquary baskets filled with bones, as among the Fang. Double-faced examples like this seem to be linked to the worship of dead twins.
Height: 68.5 cm.   Bakota (Gaboon Republic, central region).   Pierre Vérité Collection, Paris.

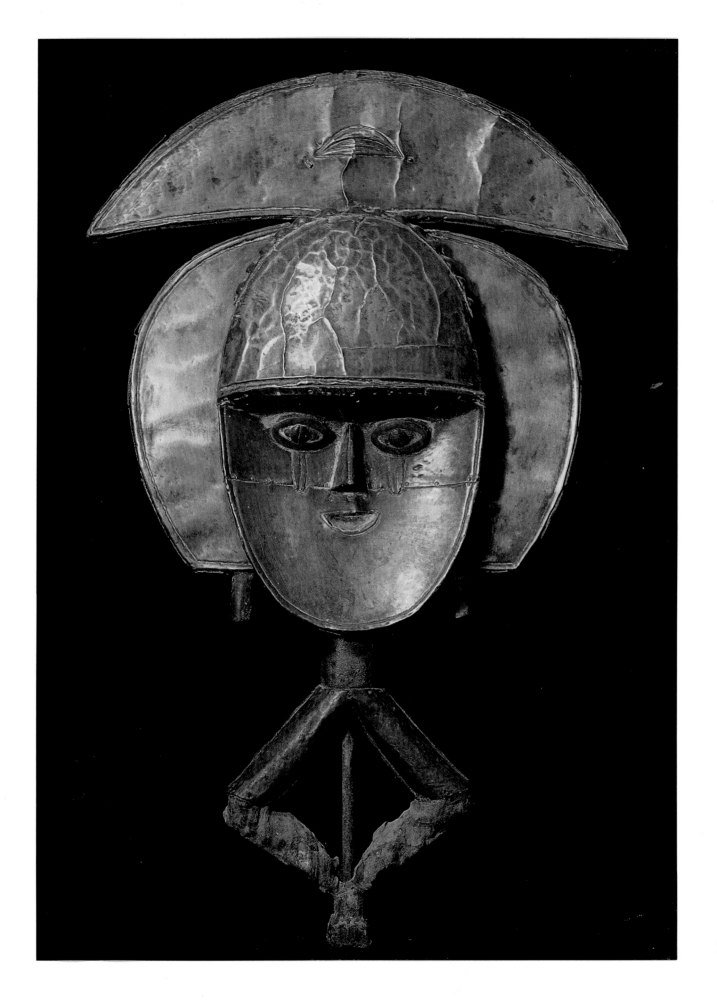

KUYU

The Kuyu live along the banks of the Kuyu river, a tributary of the right bank of the Congo, and they seem to have had a dual and conflicting worship of the snake and the panther. According to Denise Paulme, the panther was represented by a speckled drum resembling the beast's coat and containing a leopard skin. The chief himself speckled his body and dressed himself in the skin of the same animal in order to participate in its worship. As for a cult of the snake — a symbol of protection as well as a threatening reality — it is found throughout Africa and even beyond. It is represented by a cylindrical sculpture, possibly as much as one metre in height, almost entirely covered with ornamental and beautifully coloured engravings and supporting a many-faced head. During dances, only the mobile and removable part participates in the action (page 119). There are few ancient examples of this style: here, as in many other parts of West Africa, craftsmanship and tourist trade have bastardised art.

BAKONGO

When coming in contact with Bakongo sculpture, we are immediately pervaded with a feeling of human warmth which its sometimes rather brutal sensuality cannot alone explain. The statuette now at the Antwerp Museum (page 206/2) is of unusual sensual vehemence, more intense than a Maillol, no less externalised than a Bourdelle. Yet, it is far from being erotic — in fact, the idea of eroticism is meaningless in Negro Africa. The many altars dedicated to the male sex organ (Dahomey) and the exaltation of the female sex — the basic channel of life — merely state essential human needs which it would be absurd to attempt to hide. Imported Christianity — in most cases of a mediocre spirituality — did not succeed in eradicating this obvious sexual serenity. We should like again to stress the complete absence of ambiguity in African art: whether bi-sexual or dual, man-woman or woman-man (Dogon mother-and-child figures, hermaphrodite statuettes), it is always related to a strict cosmogony, never to individual eroticism. The large Bakongo fetishes, these extremely realistic figures spiked with nails and knife-blades, are, at first sight, terrifying objects, collectors of evil forces, instruments of magic 'transmission'. In the large specimens we notice that, apart from the face and hands, the body is treated almost carelessly, destined as it is from the very start to end up bristling with iron points. In the small sculptures of the same type, often finished and polished with great care, we feel a reluctance

BAPUNU. Mask of light wood. The face is whitewashed with kaolin, the lips and scarifications are painted red. The hairstyle is a triangular chignon. These masks represent the souls of the dead. They were for a long time attributed to the M'Pongwe living along the coast, but it is now established that their originators are the Bapunu or Punu.
Height: 36 cm.   Bapunu (Gaboon, western region).   Musée des Arts Africains et Océaniens, Paris.

116

on the part of the user to plant nails (page 121). This type of magic is not characteristic of all Africa, for it does not extend beyond the Mayumbe region and did not penetrate into the hinterland where the influence of the Portuguese Middle Ages and their superstitious practices still prevail.

In referring to other Bakongo 'reliquaries' with human or animal features, some of which are pervaded with much sensuous charm, Denise Paulme points out that they may well be animistic interpretations of Christian themes (copper Christs and possibly Madonnas with Child), with which the Bakongo became acquainted around the sixteenth century.

It is possible that numerous mother-and-child figures treated, in this same style, as offerings and presentations, are the result of these external influences. There is no doubt about the 'variations' on the Crucifixion theme deriving from Portuguese models: increasingly 'Africanised', they finally return to the symbolic stylisation characteristic of African art as exemplified by the *nzambi** cult symbols.

The Bakongo funeral statues in soapstone are among the best examples of freedom of form in West Africa. Legs crossed, face stamped with dreamy sadness or with resignation, they are a kind of spiritualised representation of the afterlife, and appear more Oriental than Negro in style (page 205). It is assumed that many of them were made prior to Portuguese penetration and consequently their spirit is purely African.

The beautiful Loango mask of a man (page 207) is a rare example of precise and sensitive naturalism that does not become facile or affected. Certainly inspired by a beautiful model, it becomes an archetype of its race and creates a style of which, unfortunately, only very few other examples are known; the Tervuren Museum owns its female counterpart. Although they retain the Bakongo characteristics, the plastic purity of these works seems to be imbued with a sort of free classicism rarely found among such relatively recent works. In fact, we can date them from approximately the beginning of this century.

BAYAKA — BASUKU

The Bayaka have given free vent to their imagination in the numerous initiation masks which have in common a turned-up nose. Brightly coloured, with part of the face painted white, they remind us of our clowns and we find them ludicrous rather than impressive (page 208/1 and 2). It would be interesting to discover the meaning of this trunk-like nose, unique in the whole of African sculpture. Has it a mythical origin ? Does it evoke the elephant or some other animal ?

KUYU. Large carved anthropomorphous pole surmounted by a head symbolising the protective snake. During dances, only the removable head was used. In light wood with a red-brown patina. The torso is entirely covered with geometrical and cowrie-shaped motifs set off in white. The background is blackened in places. Height: 136.5 cm. Kuyu (Republic of Congo, eastern region). Pierre Vérité Collection, Paris.

118

Certainly it is present in all these works. Generally speaking, the Basuku are considered a sub-tribe of the Bayaka, although, from an artistic point of view, the latter seem to have exercised very little influence on the former. The Basuku have produced beautifully carved helmet masks surmounted by powerfully stylised animals of a style more strict and intense than that of their neighbours. All these masks have a common use: the ritual of circumcision.

BAJOKWE

The Bajokwe have produced an enormous quantity and variety of works for varied purposes: highly idealised masks, ancestral statuettes, large initiation masks in basket-work, staffs, chairs, stools, mortars and lids. It is difficult to trace the actual African contribution to this often hybrid art, subject to Portuguese influence even as late as the eighteenth- and nineteenth-century Rococo. Today, deliberately maintained and closely supervised craftsmanship produces large quantities of sculptures which are not necessarily without interest but which aim more and more at satisfying commercial requirements. Thus, in Angola, we can witness the birth of a Bajokwe 'Christian' art with its representations of the Madonna and Child, the Nativity, the Crucifixion and the Entombment.

We must go back in time to admire the old man's mask now at the Tervuren Museum and be reassured as to the full power of its style (page 133).

During circumcision and initiation ceremonies, this mask had its counterpart representing a young girl. Maesen points out that the original religious functions of these masks have somewhat degenerated lately: they are now used in pantomimes to represent the complicated approaches between man and woman and have therefore become part of a theatrical play rather than a sacred performance. On the other hand, the monumental constructions in wicker and bark — painted or dyed — are still worshipped and surrounded with fears and interdictions. They are reserved for the secular initiation rites of young men and are publicly displayed only on these important occasions. The beautiful ancestral statuette reproduced on page 135 perfectly illustrates the lyricism of baroque forms in this style. The complicated hair-style was designed for chiefs and it is therefore assumed that this was a court art reserved for high-ranking notables.

BAPENDE

Bapende art is perhaps best known for its small amulet-masks of bone or ivory even more than for those of wood; however, while some are marvels, others should be regarded with caution.

BAKONGO. Hardwood statuette representing a man flourishing a spear. The eyes were probably once inlaid with fragments of mirror. Example of a small ' nail fetish ', probably domestic and rarely used. Height: 37 cm. *Bakongo (Republic of the Congo).* *Private collection, Paris.*

These pendants sometimes have a wonderful orange patina and faithfully reproduce the shape of the original model, the *mbuya**. Of an angular style which combines rigour and intensity of expression, the best examples of the *mbuya* achieve a merger of neighbouring styles: the purity of Bayaka forms, and the concentration and spiritual intensity of the Basuku.

The mask reproduced on page 209, used during initiation ceremonies, is one of the purest examples of this synthesis and this power.

BENA LULUA

The Bena Lulua statuette reproduced on page 210/1 belongs to the Tervuren Museum. Only a few relics of this ethnic group have reached us; we know of a local chief, Kalamba Mukenge, who, having staged a sort of *coup d'état*, tried in the second half of the nineteenth century to establish the 'cult of hemp' and abolish some of the traditional cults. He burned a great many works of art. Since then, some sculptures have reappeared, especially small mother-and-child figures. Unlike the Bakuba — their northern neighbours — the Bena Lulua produce masks which closely resemble their statuettes, with bulging foreheads and thickly painted decorations. Like the Bakuba masks, they are designed for circumcision ceremonies only.

BENA LULUA. Fertility statuette representing an obviously pregnant woman — intended to bring about and protect the birth of a child, denied till then. As in the Bakuba and N'Dengese sculptures, the body of the statuette is partly covered with refined tribal scarification.
Height: 46.5 cm. Bena Lulua (Democratic Republic of the Congo). Royal Museum of Central Africa, Tervuren.

BASONGE

Unlike Bakuba statuary art, in which ancestor worship is very prominent, Basonge art is more openly magical and even medical: it features fairly large fetishes roughly cut in wood, of a somewhat frightening appearance. These statues, many of which reach one metre in height, are hollowed out to provide reliquaries, stuffed with 'magic' substances, and often covered with all sorts of objects such as cowrie-shells, bead necklaces, nails (like the Bakongo) and antelope horns; they are also filled with such varied substances as bits of hide and cloth. Their magic power seems to be dependent on the richness and quantity of their accessories. They are supposed to keep the enemy away and even kill him. William Fagg reports that these large fetishes are considered dangerous by their users and kept outside the village as a precaution. At the same time, many small objects of the same nature are kept in the dwellings where their role is apparently only protective and beneficent.

The Basonge masks are totally different from their statues, and we can safely compare them to the round Baluba masks. Of completely different volume, they also are decorated with grooves and are painted in two or three colours (page 210/2). From the point of view of form and structure, they are among the most powerful and original products of central Africa, and they seem to be among the masks most greatly admired by Western artists; in fact, it is unusual to find so much power 'released', as it were, from such a small volume. Incidentally, Duchamp-

BALUBA. Woman holding a calabash. The statuette is called, though for no certain reason, 'the beggar'. In blackened wood, it is attributed to one of the sculptors of the village of Buli (Baluba). The original style of these statuettes, most of which are in the form of stools, reveals the definite personalisation of these works. Height: 43.5 cm. Baluba (Katanga - Dem. Republic of the Congo). Royal Museum of Central Africa, Tervuren.

Villon, one of the greatest contemporary sculptors, resorted to very similar solutions in his admirable *Cheval Majeur* — with no reference, of course, to the masks under consideration.

BAKUBA

The Bakuba are among the most 'artistic' people in the Congo inasmuch as art is integrated in their everyday life and is not the privilege of a separate caste. This leads quite naturally to works which are more ornamental than religious: there are drinking cups in hardwood decorated with one or several human faces of such delicate carving as to remind us of Chinese earthenware of the great periods. Apart from these refined examples, always in hardwood, lovingly decorated with skilful interlacing patterns and polished until they seem transparent, and apart from the extremely rare ancestral figures, the art of Bakuba masks seems rather poor; it uses perishable materials such as fibre and cloth; they seem to be intended only for circumcision and initiation rituals.

The Bakuba have the greatest respect for their historical traditions and royal personages; this accounts for the large number of famous sculptures of ancient origin. The first to be discovered was the effigy of Kata Mbula, now at the Tervuren Museum. It was undoubtedly carved in the nineteenth century, as the king reigned between 1800 and 1810. Other royal effigies discovered include those of Mikope Mbula and Bope Kena. William Fagg is of the opinion that the statue of Shamba Bolongongo acquired by the British Museum in 1909 might be a copy made in the eighteenth century. If we compare their styles and techniques, we come to the conclusion that these works are more representative of the sculptors who made them than of the models who inspired them. Each king represented is identified by his special attributes, although the pose in all these works is the same, and they all have the same distant expression of concentration. As for their meaning, let us quote Maesen in *Umbangu* :

BALUBA. Large helmet-mask in blackened wood. The face, of great purity of form, is framed by braids and horns. Remarkable 'winding' composition in which all the details — eyes, eyebrows, mouth — are emphasised. An outstanding example of this particular style, already so rich in masterpieces.
Height: 39 cm.   Baluba (Democratic Republic of the Congo).   Royal Museum of Central Africa, Tervuren.

126

'The actual function of these statues is known only in part. According to recent findings, the effigy of the king, carved during his lifetime, was placed beside his death-bed in order that it might absorb the metaphysical power of the dying 'earthly king'. During the period of seclusion imposed before his investiture, the successor was made to lie beside the statue and received by incubation the power transmitted by his predecessor.'

BABEMBE

The Babembe, who settled to the north of Lake Tanganyika, can be singled out for their powerful and architectural style. We know of a whole series of portraits of royal ancestors, and the work which we reproduce is undoubtedly the most powerful of all: archetype of this brutal and at the same time radiant style, it is one of the most mysterious and, in our opinion, remarkable masterpieces of African art (page 212/1). The Babembe have also a type of helmet-mask called *Kalunga*. These masks are essentially 'visionary', the plastic idea of the human face being almost entirely confined to its visual function. Here, abstract invention is obvious and unequivocal — yet, true abstraction always draws power from real life.

N'DENGESE — WAREGA — BAMBOLE

Little is known of the imposing N'Dengese statues with scarified bodies, always marked with great dignity (page 131). The rare specimens known are old, dating at least from the nineteenth century. Their style certainly derives from that of the Bakuba, but the N'Dengese have an original conception of sculpture which distinguishes them. We do not know whether the carved effigies represent ancestors or deceased notables.

The Bwame society from which Warega or Balega art seems to derive, comprises several male and female ranks. These ranks are illustrated by small masks and statuettes of ivory, with a patina ranging from pale yellow to dark orange-red. Others, in bone, are of a lighter shade; still others are of wood and often have several faces enhanced by a white colouring. These latter call to mind the Bakwele masks of the Gaboon. These masks, statuettes and insignia are fastened to the shoulders of their owners during ritual dances. The large 'front-view' ivory masks (page 214/2) worn over the face are extremely rare. We know of a few specimens in very light wood, very expressive and of similar style (page 215).

BAKUBA. Portrait of King Shamba Bolongongo, in very hard brown wood. This is the image of one of the most famous kings who reigned about 1600 and who established the custom, which has been followed ever since, of these portrait-statues. We suspect that this statue was not made during the king's lifetime, but is an eighteenth-century copy.
Height: 54.5 cm.   Bakuba-Bushongo kingdom (Dem. Republic of the Congo).   British Museum, London.

It is believed that this important society assigns ivory to the higher ranks and positions, just as elsewhere bronze prevails over wood, and gold over brass. The striking art of the Warega impresses us by its mystery: we refer to a minute statuette with arms thrown upwards in a silent cry; hardly ever has such intensity been expressed in so small a statue. It was reproduced in the special edition of *Musée Vivant* published in 1948 (Ratton Collection).

Maesen points out, quite rightly, that while it is true that most African statues are more or less directly linked to ancestor worship and to the transfer of power into living beings — their worldly successors — it is nonetheless rare that such objects should be endowed with powers of initiation and revelation. This, however, is the case with the Bambole effigies (page 214/1) used exclusively for this type of ritual. Carved with great determination — sharp angles, hollow faces — technically they remind us of the Bakwele figures and some of the Warega statuettes.

BALUBA

The classicism, charm and apparent humanity of Baluba art, as famous as that of the Ivory Coast Baule, have long ago conquered lovers of gentle but deeply expressive sculpture. There is no doubt that the finest examples of this art, such as the ancestor's face at the Antwerp Museum or a similar fragment at the Stuttgart Museum (page 212/2), can attain great concentration and spiritual radiance.

The Baluba masks alone are of an infinite variety. Some of them have the shape of a half-sphere with concentric grooving starting off from the mouth and surrounding the eyes. Others, like the Tervuren helmet-mask (pages 126 and 127), a masterpiece of Baluba art, are probably among the finest in Negro Africa. The beauty of the stools supported by caryatids far exceeds their domestic and even ornamental purpose and attains, in some instances, deep concentration and even mysticism. This style, which derives from Baluba classicism, is derivative and yet original, and proves, once again, the identity of art and of the man who creates it. Some of these stools carved by one or more sculptors of Buli village, are supported either by two figures — male and female — or by a kneeling woman with huge hands in the shape of palm leaves. The opposition of planes often intersecting at right angles enhances the austerity of these sculptures, meant to be of a peaceful and domestic nature, and bestows power upon them. William Fagg distinguishes two 'masters' in Buli: one carved hardwood, the other, a softer material. Whatever the case may be, no more than ten works of this origin are known, and it is quite

N'DENGESE. *Royal statuette in hardwood: the face has a shiny black patina; the torso and arms are entirely covered with scarifications containing Bakuba decorative motifs. White marks remain in the grooves. More powerful in style than the Bushongo royal statues, it represents a symbol, an archetype of divine and earthly power, rather than the portrait of a specific living king.*
Height: 53 cm. N'Dengese (Democratic Republic of the Congo). Royal Museum of Central Africa, Tervuren.

likely that late copies and even fakes already exist. The Tervuren 'begging woman' quite rightly holds first place in this amazing series (pages 124 and 125).

BAROTSE

North of the Zambezi, the Barotse are known mainly for their oval wooden dishes with decorated lids representing a variety of animals: elephants, birds, etc. The Mbunda, in the same area, have very expressive masks with huge foreheads and chubby cheeks which are used at new moon ceremonies.

MAKONDE

The Makonde, who live along the northern Mozambique frontier, produce masks considered to be the most realistic of all African sculptures. Unfortunately, this style is fading away and is degenerating into flabby curves.

BUKOBA

The Bukoba in Tanzania have achieved great skill in iron-craft, of which the stylised bull — a highly abstract work — is a striking example (page 216/1). It can be seen at the Linden-Museum, Stuttgart. One cannot help thinking of Picasso's famous series of engravings: starting off with a wholly realistic bull with tail, horns, hair, eyes and muzzle, firmly planted on its legs and hoofs, and proceeding by analytical and simplifying stages, Picasso arrives at a purity of line which ends up with 'the idea of the bull'.

MANGBETU

The Mangbetu, who live near the Egyptian-Sudan frontier, above the Welle River, have found plastic expression in a rich and complex ornamental art. Apart from statues, examples of which are rare, they have made two-faced drums, statuettes and boxes surmounted by narrow heads, *tapas** made of fig-tree bark, and cloth. They also have portable harps ending up with one or several figures and pottery featuring female faces well worthy of their proximity to the Nile. The elongated shape of the faces decorating the pottery is drawn from actual models: in fact, it is customary among the Mangbetu to deform the skulls of babies by means of cloth strips so as to give them a tubular shape.

BAJOKWE. Mask in brown wood with brass rings hanging from the ears. This mask, powerful in its severity, represents the old man during initiation dances performed in the course of circumcision ceremonies. Height: 23.5 cm. Bajokwe (Democratic Republic of the Congo). Royal Museum of Central Africa, Tervuren.

AZANDE

Azande art consists of a wide range of decorated pottery, musical instruments, harps and ivory horns decorated with human faces. Only few representational statuettes have reached us and we can only regret that the small figure reproduced on page 216/2, radiant with life, is almost unique.

BAJOKWE. Ancestor statue in hardwood with black patina, that looks almost lacquered. The monumental head-dress, symbol of virility and of social power, bestows beauty and dignity upon this extremely pure and strict example of a type of sculpture too often anecdotal and over-ornate.

Height: 37.5 cm.   Bajokwe (Congo or Angola frontier region).   René Rasmussen Collection, Paris.

The illustrations that follow are grouped together according to their geographical locations:

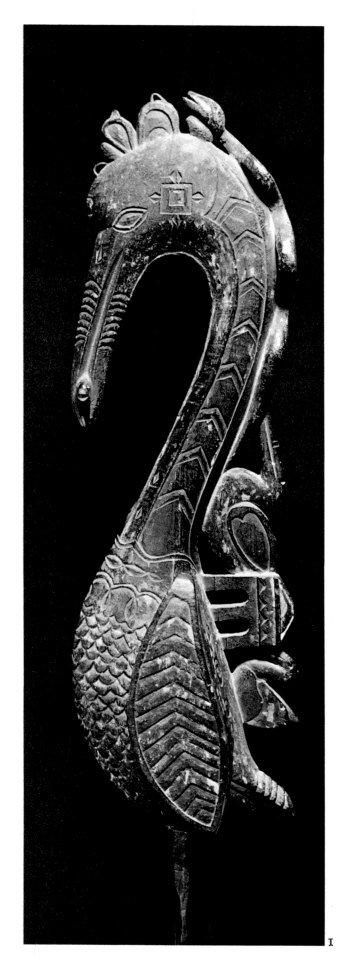

Preceding page. BAGA. Large shoulder-mask called *Nimba,* usually dressed in a fibre costume. A fertility mask, it is invoked during the rice harvesting or by women – both pregnant and infertile – soliciting its help and protection.
In wood, height: 127 cm. Baga (Republic of Guinea). Maurice Nicaud Collection, Paris.

1. BAGA. Wooden bird with dark brown patina enhanced with lighter colours inside the carving. Used during agricultural ceremonies for the cultivation of rice.
Height: 65 cm. Baga (Republic of Guinea). R. Rasmussen Collection, Paris.

2. BAGA. Wooden bird painted in orange and white. Two little birds are on its wings. Used during the same ceremonies as the preceding object.
Height: 73 cm. Baga (Republic of Guinea). Maurice Nicaud Collection, Paris.

3. BAGA. Wooden mask painted in orange, black and white. Lower jaw movable.
Height: 90 cm. Baga (Republic of Guinea). Clamagirand Collection, Paris.

1

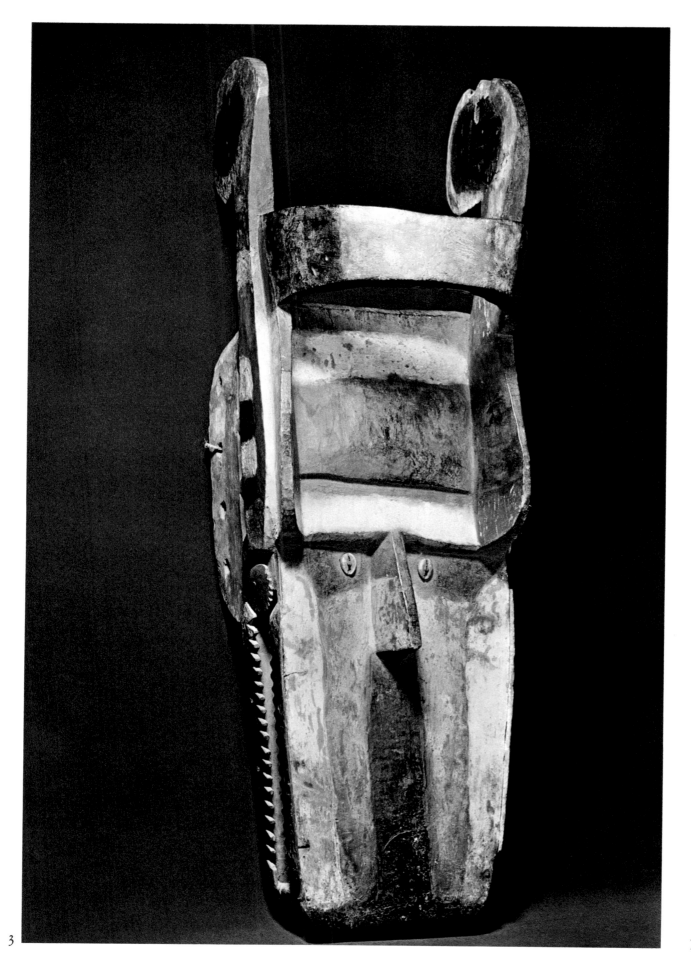

1. KISSI. Large head carved in soapstone. Used for ancestor-worship but also for divination.
Height: 26 cm. Kissi (Republic of Guinea). Museum of Primitive Art, New York.

2. KISSI. Funeral stone called *nomoli,* carved in soft soapstone and representing a seated man in an attitude of deep concentration.
Height: 26 cm. Kissi (Republic of Guinea). Musée des Arts Africains et Océaniens, Paris.

3. KISSI. Funeral figure of soapstone *(nomoli)*. A couple, apparently under the protection of a mythical ancestor. Height: 32 cm. Kissi (Sierra Leone Republic). Pitt Rivers Museum, Oxford.

1. MENDE. Large statue in blackened wood. Is endowed with healing power and transmits the wishes of spirits through the medium of shaman priestesses.
Height: 117,5 cm. Mende (Sierre Leone Republic).
British Museum, London.

2. MENDE. Funeral figure of soapstone (*nomoli*).
Represents a horseman. The horse has been mutilated.
Height: 11.5 cm. Mende (Sierre Leone Republic).
Museum of Art, Baltimore.

3. MENDE. Wooden helmet-mask of the Mende Bundu female secret society.
Height: 40 cm. Mende (Sierra Leone Republic). Musée de l'Institut Français d'Afrique Noire, Dakar.

1

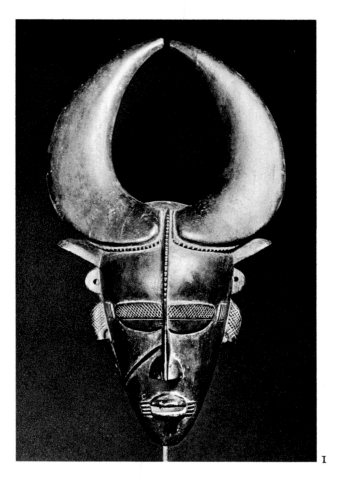

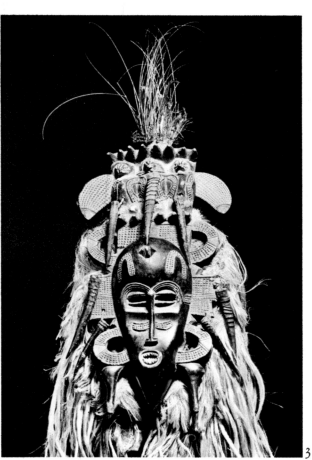

1. SENUFO. Mask of darkened wood with a shiny patina, surmounted by large flat horns. Senufo sub-ethnic group (Nafana), east of Korhogo.
Height: 42 cm. Senufo (Ivory Coast Republic). Musée des Arts Africains et Océaniens, Paris.

2. SENUFO. The door of a hut. Made of dark brown wood, it is decorated with animals and masks typical of this style.
Dimensions: 135 × 79 cm. Senufo (Ivory Coast Republic). André Held Collection, Ecublens (Switzerland).

3. SENUFO. Wooden mask, exceptionally complete example of the classical prototype of Senufo masks. The forehead is surrounded by gazelle horns.
Height: 36 cm. Senufo (Ivory Coast Republic). Museum of Primitive Art, New York.

4. SENUFO. Wooden helmet-crest in openwork with human and animal decorations typical of the Senufo. Double face with varied motifs.
Dimensions: 133.5 × 71 cm. Senufo (Ivory Coast Republic). André Held Collection, Ecublens.

4

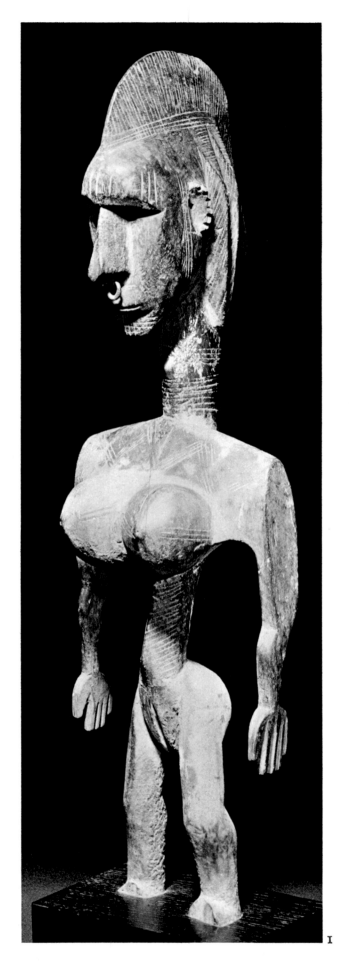

1. BAMBARA. Female statuette of dark wood, probably representing fertility.
Height: 70 cm. Bambara (Mali Republic). Henri Kamer Collection, Cannes.

2. BAMBARA. Mask of light-coloured wood, very eroded. This specimen brings to mind the so-called 'Buguni Queen' style from which it very likely derives.
Height: 29 cm. Bambara-Buguni (Mali Republic). Private collection, Cannes.

3. BAMBARA. Mask of blackened wood, surmounted, between what might be fingers or horns, by a female ancestor figure. Used during ceremonies for the initiation of young boys.
Height: 68 cm. Bambara (Mali Republic). Pierre Vérité Collection, Paris.

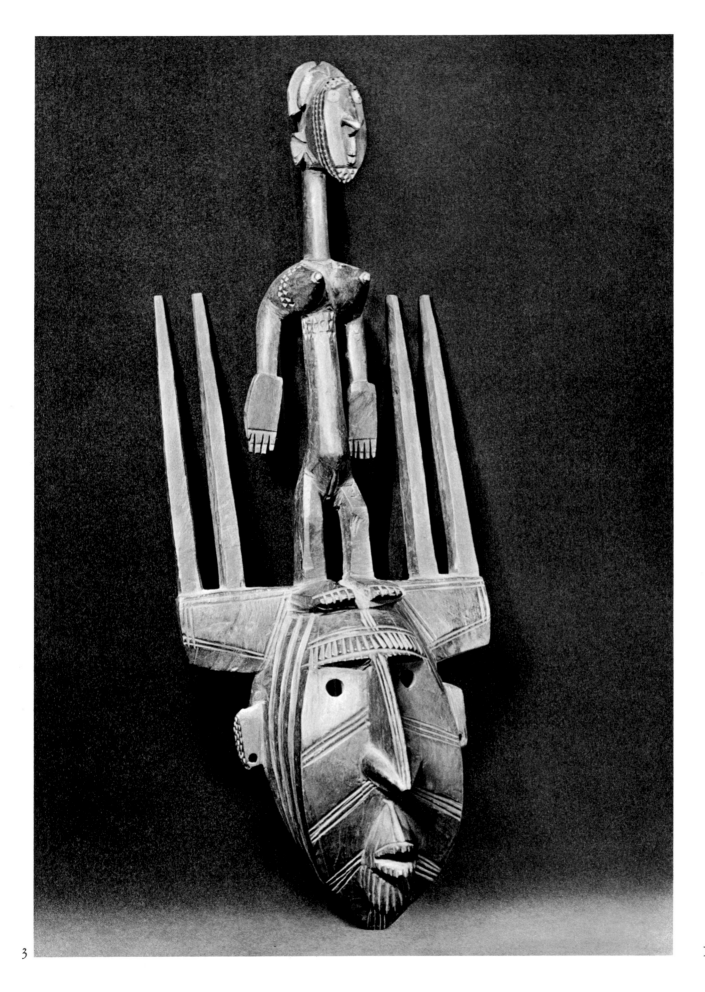

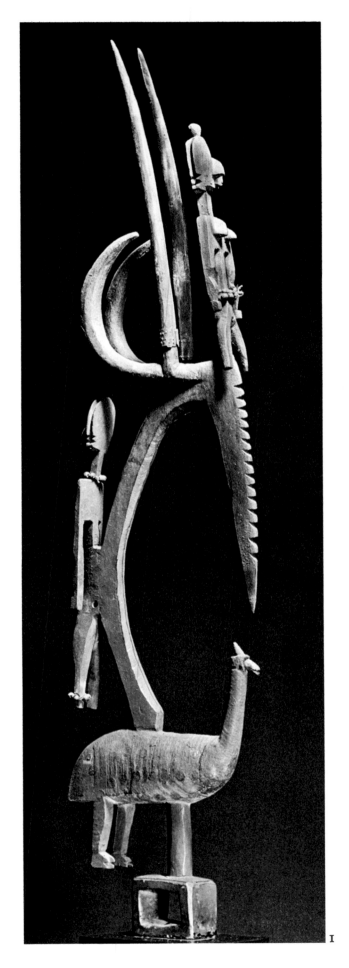

1. BAMBARA. *Chi wara* antelope. Crest of dark wood with red highlight. Among the numerous variations on this theme, this example is extremely balanced and spontaneous. Used during agricultural rituals.
Height: 75 cm. Bambara (Mali Republic). M. Nicaud Collection, Paris.

2. BAMBARA. Wooden crest representing a small antelope with inverted horns. Used during agricultural rituals.
Height: 45 cm. Bambara (Mali Republic). Clamagirand Collection, Paris.

3. BAMBARA. Large mask of black wood enhanced by small pieces of cut-out metal. Animal synthesis (bat, antelope?).
Height: 79 cm. Bambara (Mali Republic). Musée des Arts Africains et Océaniens, Paris.

1. DOGON. Large wooden statue, very eroded, representing a bird-seed grinder, a mythical ancestor in her role as a provider of food.
Height: 98 cm. Dogon (Mali Republic). Private collection, Cannes.

2. DOGON. Wooden torso, very eroded, fragment of an ancestor statuette.
Height: 27 cm. Dogon (Mali Republic). Private collection, Cannes.

3. DOGON. Ritual object of blackened wood with a thick patina. This group represents the eight fundamental ancestors supporting the world.
Height: 43,5 cm. Dogon (Mali Republic). Museum of Primitive Art, New York.

1. DOGON. Large statue of natural wood representing an ancestor figure.
Height: 110 cm. Dogon (Mali Republic). Henri Kamer Collection, Cannes.

2. DOGON. Granary door of natural wood representing 'father-crocodile' and *tellem* figures.
Dimensions: 75 × 46 cm. Dogon (Mali Republic). Private collection, Cannes.

3. DOGON. Female statuette of natural wood representing an ancestor figure grinding rice.
Height: 49 cm. Dogon (Mali Republic). Private collection, Paris.

4. DOGON. Large ancestor statue of natural wood with the classical Dogon face.
Height: 71 cm. Dogon (Mali Republic). Henri Kamer Collection, Paris.

1

3

4

1. DOGON. Fragment of a mask of natural light-coloured wood, probably the top of a plank-mask representing an ancestor.
Height: 120 cm. Dogon (Mali Republic). Private collection, Paris.

2. DOGON. Small horseman of eroded wood, probably very old. Mythical figure of an ancestor on horseback.
Height: 29 cm. Dogon (Mali Republic). Hélène Kamer Collection, Paris.

3. DOGON. Wooden statuette representing a seated woman holding a child.
Height: 57,5 cm. Dogon (Mali Republic). University Museum, Philadelphia.

1. BOBO-FING. Helmet-mask of light wood with cut-out geometrical decorations painted in black and white.
Height: 118 cm. Bobo-Fing (Upper Volta Republic). Musée des Arts Africains et Océaniens, Paris.

2. BOBO. Helmet-mask of light wood painted in red and white. The face is surmounted by a half-disc reminiscent of the Roman centurion helmets.
Height: 73.5 cm. Bobo (Upper Volta Republic). Musée des Arts Africains et Océaniens, Paris.

3. BOBO. Large mask of natural wood with, in places, lightly painted geometrical motifs in black, grey and blue. Represents the roan antelope. The curve of the horns sets off the inverted curve of the face.
Height: 110 cm. Bobo (Upper Volta Republic). Maurice Nicaud Collection, Paris.

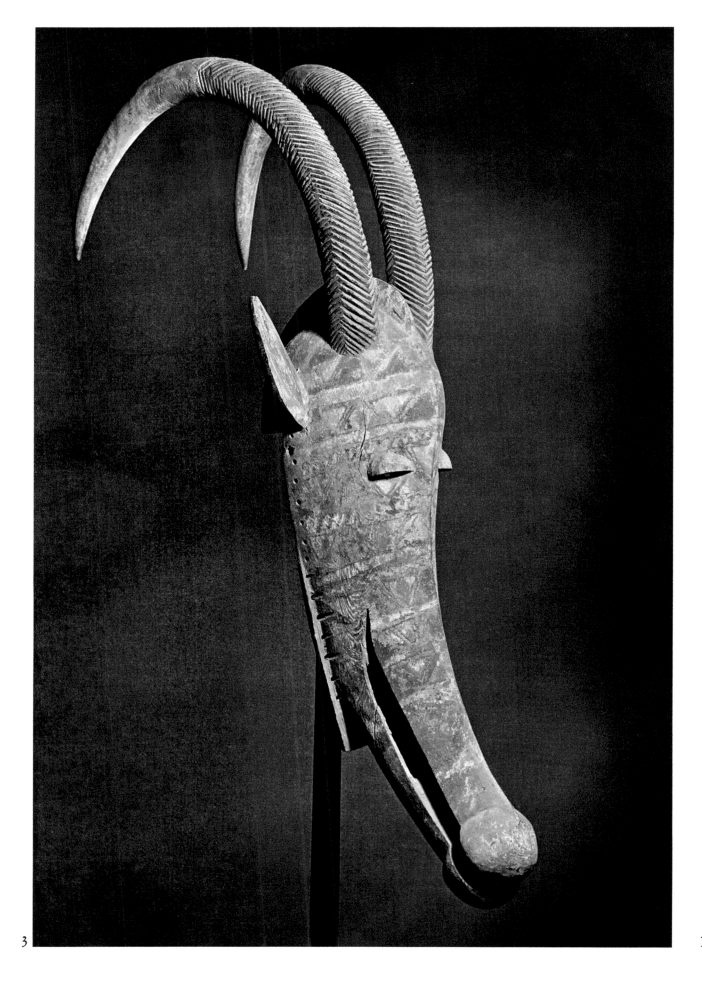

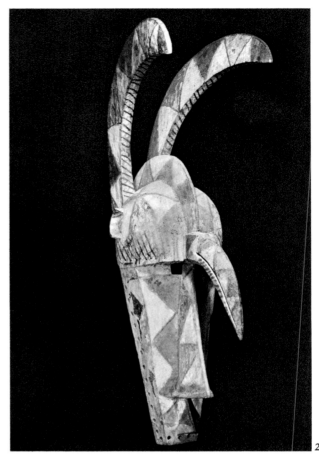

1. BOBO. Wooden plank-mask, a classical example of Bobo art. Moon-shaped face with beak, surmounted by a geometrically decorated flat superstructure.
Height: 137 cm. Bobo (Upper Volta Republic). André Held Collection, Ecublens.

2. BOBO. Helmet-mask of light wood with red, blue and white ornamental motifs. Horns curve forwards.
Height: 92 cm. Bobo (Upper Volta Republic). Musée des Arts Africains et Océaniens, Paris.

3. LOBI. Fragment of a female torso of wood, badly eroded.
Height: 54 cm. Lobi (Upper Volta Republic). Musée des Arts Africains et Océaniens, Paris.

1

1

2

3

4

1. LOBI. Statuette of badly eroded wood. Ancestor figure.
Height: 69 cm. Lobi (Upper Volta Republic). Maurice Nicaud Collection, Paris.

2. LOBI. Head of hardwood of a rough and forceful cut. Head supported by a very long neck.
Height: 39 cm. Lobi (Upper Volta Republic). André Held Collection, Ecublens.

3. DAN. Mask of polished wood with 'lacquered' black patina. The face, of great purity, has half-closed eyes and is surrounded by plaits of natural hair.
Height: 22 cm. Dan-Yakuba (Ivory Coast Republic). Henri Kamer Collection, Cannes.

4. DAN. Mask of polished dark wood with reddish patina in the hollows. Round, wide-opened eyes. Worn by young men during inter-village races. (See J. Girard).
Height: 25 cm. Dan-Yakuba (Ivory Coast Republic). Musée des Arts Africains et Océaniens, Paris.

5. NGERE-WOBE. Wooden mask in human and animal shape. Two rows of tubular eyes covered with metal discs. Lower part ends in a curved beak surrounded by a beard made of natural hair.
Height: 53 cm. Ngere-Wobe (Republic of Liberia). Peabody Archaeological and Ethnographical Museum, Harvard University.

5

161

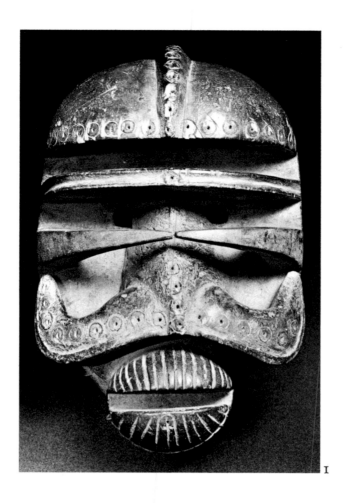

1. NGERE-WOBE. Wooden mask with a dark brown patina, enhanced with metal nail-heads. Points bent towards the eyes.
Height: 28 cm. Ngere-Wobe (Ivory Coast Republic). Henri Kamer Collection, Cannes.

2. NGERE-WOBE. Wooden mask, called *Gla*. The beard and hair around the face are of twisted raffia. Teeth are represented by metal points.
Height: 21 cm. Ngere-Wobe (Ivory Coast Republic). Private collection, Cannes.

3. TOMA. Large wooden mask. A flat face, with no mouth, and projecting nose. The eyes are represented by two very small slits. The representation of a supernatural being, the ritual function of which is unknown.
Height: 57 cm. Toma (Ivory Coast Republic). Musée Municipal, Angoulême.

4. NGERE-WOBE. Mask of dark wood, whitened around the eyes and nose. Prominent forehead. The face is concave from the eyebrows to the mouth.
Height: 25 cm. Ngere-Wobe (Ivory Coast Republic). Musée des Arts Africains et Océaniens, Paris.

1. BAULE. Wooden statue with wide, haloed forehead. Ancestor figure. The face ends with a beard divided into three tresses.
Height: 62 cm. Baule (Ivory Coast Republic). Henri Kamer Collection, Cannes.

2. BAULE. Mask of hardwood with 'lacquered' black patina. Face surmounted by three small heads in the same style.
Height: 42 cm. Baule (Ivory Coast Republic). Maurice Nicaud Collection, Paris.

3. BAULE. Wooden mask. The face, archaic in style, is topped with a sort of comb. Decorated with a few brass nail-heads.
Height: 32 cm. Baule (Ivory Coast Republic). Musée des Arts Africains et Océaniens, Paris.

1. BAULE. Wooden statuette with a granular, nearly black patina. This ancestor figure is one of the best examples of the 'classicism' of this style.
Height: 38,5 cm. Baule (Ivory Coast Republic). R. Duperrier Collection, Paris.

2. BAULE. Small statue of dark wood with a lighter, grainy patina, representing an ancestor seated on a chief's stool (Ashanti-Baule style).
Height 42 cm. Baule (Ivory Coast Republic). Royal Museum of Central Africa, Tervuren (Belgium).

3. BAULE. Round mask of badly eroded wood. Flat, moon-shaped face surmounted by horns.
Height: 98 cm. Baule (Ivory Coast Republic). René Van der Straete Collection, Brussels.

1

1. BAULE. Wooden statuette, nearly black, with a shiny patina. Representation of a round-faced ancestor. The limbs fit into one another like telescope sections. Rare example among the Baule, usually so respectful of form.
Height: 50 cm. Baule-Agni (?) (Ivory Coast Republic). J. Roudillon Collection, Paris.

2. BAULE. Large mask of natural wood, badly eroded. Archaic type of the classical *Guli* mask.
Height: 124 cm. Baule (Ivory Coast Republic). Musée des Arts Africains et Océaniens, Paris.

3. BAULE-YAURE. Mask of very dark brown wood with a shiny patina. The head is topped with a wader pecking in a cup. A similar bird facing it has disappeared. Metal triangles under the eyes.
Height: 40 cm. Baule-Yaure (Ivory Coast Republic). Musée des Arts Africains et Océaniens, Paris.

1

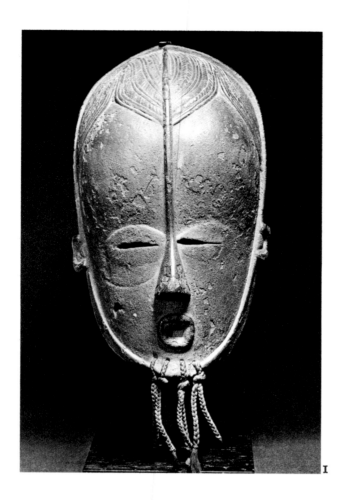

1. GURO. Mask of blackened wood with rough patina. The forehead is divided by a cicatrice. Plaited beard of natural hair.
Height: 28 cm. Guro (Ivory Coast Republic). Musée des Arts Africains et Océaniens, Paris.

2. GURO. Wooden mask with black 'lacquered' patina and red geometrical designs. This animal synthesis – antelope and wolf? – is typical of this style.
Height: 43 cm. Guro (Ivory Coast Republic). Private collection, Ecublens, Switzerland.

3. KRINJABO. Fragment of a funeral terracotta of the Assinian region. Very expressive face surmounted by a coiffure in the shape of a crown.
Height: 20 cm. Krinjabo (Lower Ivory Coast). Musée des Arts Africains et Océaniens, Paris.

4. KRINJABO. Fragment of a funeral terracotta representing an old man's head.
Height: 18 cm. Krinjabo (Lower Ivory Coast). André Held Collection, Ecublens.

1. ASHANTI. Door of a hut of very dark brown wood decorated with a big fish eating a small fish, which is also claimed by an ox-pecker.
Dimensions: 157×58.5 cm. Ashanti (Republic of Ghana). Musée des Arts Africains et Océaniens, Paris.

2. ASHANTI. Doll of blackened and shiny wood. The face, perfectly round, is attached to the small cylindrical body by a very long neck. These fertility dolls, called *Akua ba,* are carried by pregnant women to ensure the birth of a healthy child.
Height: 37 cm. Ashanti (Republic of Ghana). Clamagirand Collection, Paris.

3. ASHANTI. Large bronze receptacle called *Kuduo,* cast in the *cire-perdue* technique and decorated with floral motifs. The lid represents a scene of the royal court, the king surrounded by his musicians. A funerary object, it was filled with gold dust and buried beside the deceased king.
Height: 31 cm. Ashanti (Republic of Ghana). Ghana Museum.

4. ASHANTI. Wooden statuette partly whitened with kaolin. The face brings to mind the style of the *Akua ba* and of the Ashanti funeral terracottas. The arms are inserted but are not movable.
Height: 39 cm. Ashanti (Republic of Ghana). Musée des Arts Africains et Océaniens, Paris.

1

1.   EWE. Bovid mask of terracotta burnished with graphite, giving the impression of darkened bronze. One of the few pieces of sculpture created in Togo.
Height: 22,8 cm. Ewe (Republic of Togo). Museum of Primitive Art, New York.

2.   YORUBA. Gelede mask of brown wood set off in grey, ochre and red. The face is topped with a daringly asymmetrical head-dress.
Height: 32 cm. Yoruba-Keitu (Dahomey Republic). André Held Collection, Ecublens.

3.   YORUBA. Oshe-Shango group of light, painted wood, ending in a stick. Carried during ceremonies for the worship of Shango, god of thunder and lightning.
Height: 57 cm. Yoruba (Nigerian Federation). French Institute Museum of Negro Africa, Dakar.

2

1. YORUBA. Horseman of ivory with a light purplish-blue patina. The man on horseback carries the double Edan cult symbol.
Height: 30 cm. Yoruba (Nigerian Federation). British Museum, London.

2. YORUBA. Oshe-Shango female figure of natural well-polished wood. The face is topped with the double axe, ritual Shango insignia.
Height: 59.3 cm. Yoruba (Nigerian Federation). British Museum, London.

3. NOK. Large head of light-coloured terracotta. In the middle of the smooth and bulging forehead, there is a little disc in relief. Stylised coiffure. One of the major pieces produced by this ancient culture.
Height: 25 cm. Nok (Nigerian Federation). Nigerian Museums.

1

1. IFE. Head of a queen in red-pink terracotta. The face is scarified with parallel lines.
Height: 26,5 cm. Ife (Nigerian Federation). Nigerian Museums.

2. IFE. Head of a queen in bronze with green-lacquered 'excavation' patina.
Height: 24 cm. Ife (Nigerian Federation). Nigerian Museums.

3. BENIN. Small bronze plaque cast in the *cire perdue* technique. Represents a young girl carrying a leopard-shaped aquamanile on her left shoulder. Background decorated with floral motifs. One of the few female representations in this style.
Height: 45 cm. Benin (Nigerian Federation). A. Schwarz Collection, Amsterdam.

4. IFE. Large royal helmet-mask of bronze with brown patina. The slits under the eyes allow for vision.
Height: 32,5 cm. Ife (Nigerian Federation). Nigerian Museums.

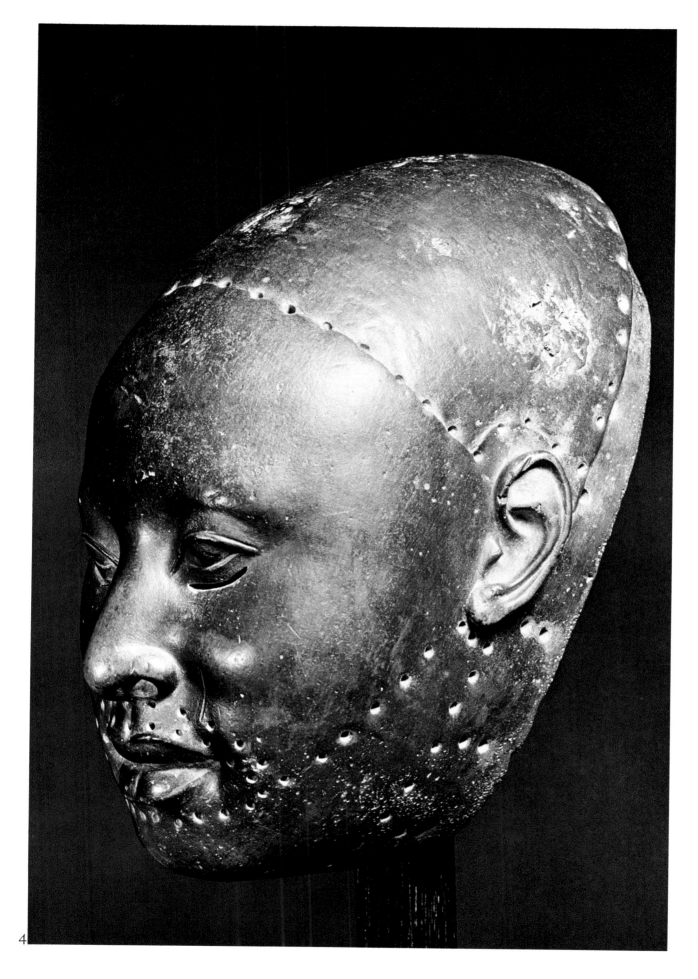

1. JEBBA. Large bronze statue with brown patina. Representation of an archer in hunting clothes carrying on his back a quiver full of arrows. The fore-arms and the bow are missing. He seems to wear a woven tunic with parallel strips or a chain-plated armour.
Height: 92 cm. Jebba. Lower Nigerian bronze industry. (Nigerian Federation). Collection of the Jebba Dagacin (chief).

2. BENIN. Head of dark green-brown bronze. The neck is encircled with superimposed necklaces. On the top of the head, there is a round hole, presumably to hold a carved elephant's tusk. Votive figure of the Benin City court (about eighteenth century).
Height: 39 cm. Benin (Nigerian Federation). Musée des Antiquités Nationales, Saint-Germain-en-Laye.

3. BENIN. Bronze plaque with bas-relief representing an Oba accompanied by two of his servants. Background decorated with floral motifs. These plaques were affixed to the posts and walls of the galleries of the royal palace in Benin City.
Height: 52.2 cm. Benin (Nigerian Federation). British Museum, London.

1

1. BENIN. Bronze aquamanile in the shape of a ram. Water was poured onto the royal hands through the holes in the nose.
Height: 33,7 cm. Benin (Nigerian Federation). British Museum, London.

2. BENIN. Bronze plaque representing a notable or a Portuguese soldier. The prominent and hooked nose deliberately emphasises the foreign character of the model.
Height: 49,9 cm. Benin (Nigerian Federation). British Museum, London.

3. BENIN. Horseman of cast brass, in *cire perdue* technique. Probably represents a messenger from the north coming to the Benin court. He seems to be riding a mule.
Height: 47 cm. Benin (Nigerian Federation). British Museum, London.

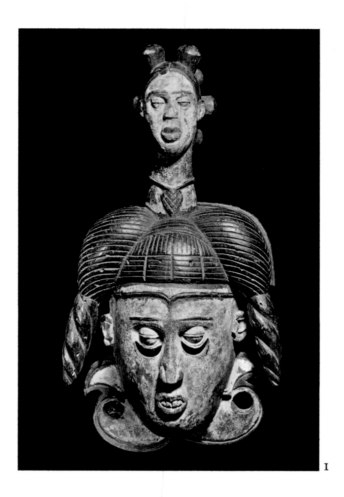

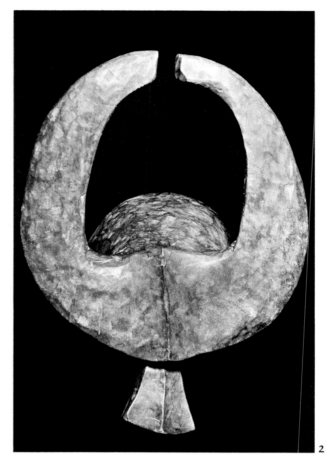

1. IBIBIO. Wooden mask surmounted by a smaller replica. Relatively light, it is painted in black and white. Height: 57 cm. Ibibio (Nigerian Federation). Museum of Primitive Art, New York.

2. MAMA. Wooden mask with brown patina and pink-red glint. An almost abstract synthesis of a bovid. Height: 36 cm. Mama (Nigerian Federation). Charles Ratton Collection, Paris.

3. IBO. Sculpture in grey-green basalt. These funeral figures, engraved rather than carved, were planted in the ground in large groups.
Height: 108 cm. Ibo Ogoja (Nigerian Federation). Nigerian Museums.

4. AFO. Mother and child in blackened wood with tribal scarifications. The seated mother holds her child with a gesture of withdrawal if not rejection.
Height: 58 cm. Afo (Nigerian Federation). Horniman Museum, London.

1. NUPE. Wooden mask of the Nupe tribe (northern Nigeria).
Height: 66,5 cm. Nupe (Nigerian Federation). British Museum, London.

2. EPE. Wooden mask. Round-eyed face surmounted by a cut-out crest.
Height: 100 cm. Epe-Yoruba (Nigerian Federation). Nigerian Museums.

3. IJO. Wooden screen painted in brown and set off in white. Funeral composition representing seated figures and small replicas of masks typical of this ethnic group. (The mask representing the spirit of water is recognisable on the upper edge.)
Height: 125 cm. Kalabari Ijo (Nigerian Federation). British Museum, London.

1

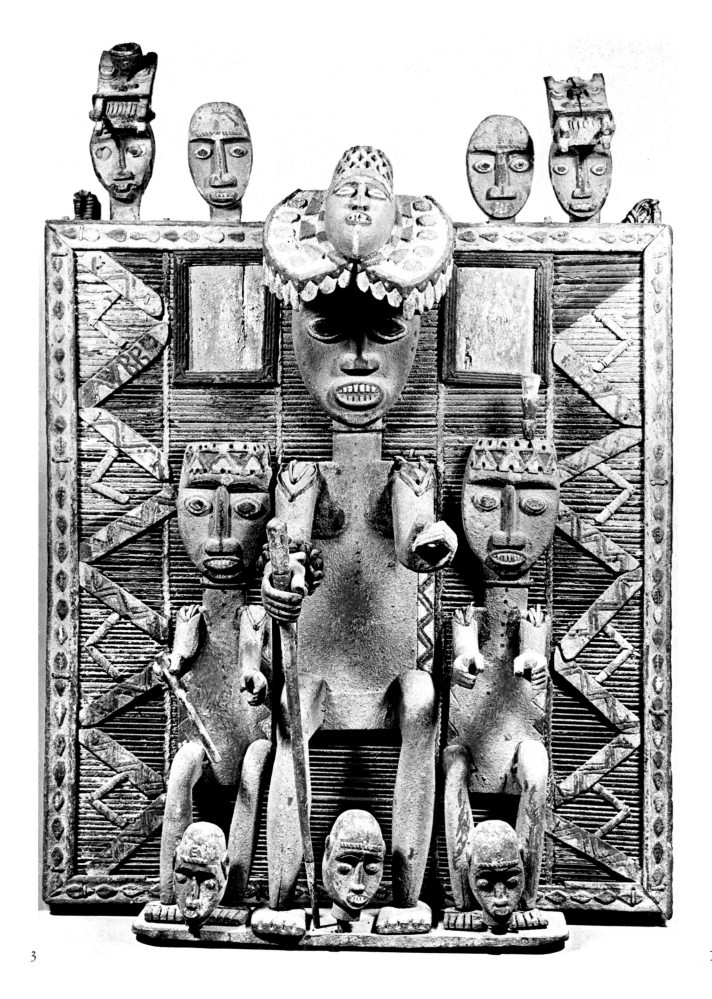

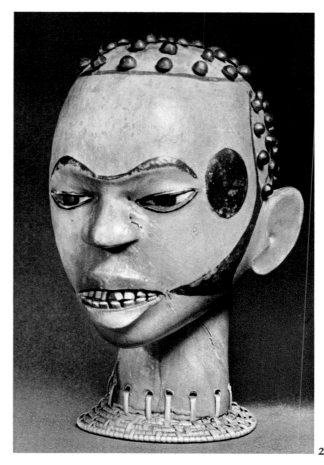

1. ORON. Ancestor statuette. The wood, badly eroded at the base, implies that these figures were planted in the ground. Probably represents a mythical ancestor.
Height: 93 cm. Oron (Nigerian Federation). Nigerian Museums.

2. EKOI. Cap mask of wood covered with natural antelope skin, decorated in black and set on a small inverted basket which allowed it to be worn during ritual dances.
Height: 27.9 cm. Ekoi (Nigerian Federation). Museum of Primitive Art, New York.

3. SAO-KOTOKO. Grey terracotta statuette representing an ancestor with arms outstretched. Scarifications on neck.
Height: 36 cm. Sao-Kotoko, Buta-Kabira (Chad Republic). National Chad Museum, Fort-Lamy.

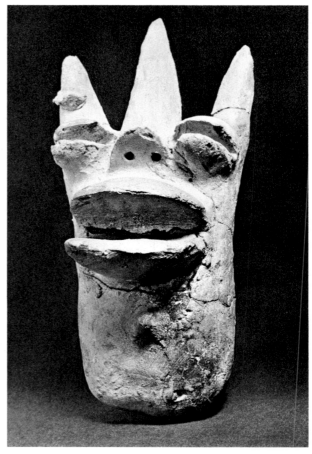

1. SAO. Ancestor head in pinkish-red terracotta, called *Afade*. Elongated face ending up in a pointed beard.
Height: 20,3 cm. Sao-Afade (Chad Republic). Lafaille Natural History Museum, La Rochelle.

2. SAO-KOTOKO. Fragment of human head in terracotta. Face with protruding lips and eyelids, surmounted by three horns.
Height: 19 cm. Sao-Kotoko, Buta-Kabira (Chad Republic). National Chad Museum, Fort-Lamy.

3. SAO-KOTOKO. Terracotta head surmounted by a sort of horn, prolongation of the bridge of the nose.
Height: 20,3 cm. Sao-Kotoko, Buta-Kabira (Chad Republic). National Chad Museum, Fort-Lamy.

4. BAMILEKE. Wooden statuette, reddened in places. Represents a crouching ancestor holding a vessel of offerings between his knees. These statuettes were placed on the floor of the galleries surrounding the large dwellings of the chiefs.
Height: 73 cm. Bamileke (Republic of Cameroon). Museum of Ethnography, Berlin.

1. BAMILEKE. Wooden mask whitewashed with kaolin. Face with prominent features ending up in a pointed chin. Hair-dress represented by numerous cylindrical protuberances.
Height: 26.2 cm. Bamileke, Bameta (Republic of Cameroon). Linden-Museum, Stuttgart.

2. DUALA. Bovid mask of wood lacquered in white, orange and black. This type of mask has now completely disappeared from coastal Cameroon art.
Height: 97.2 cm. Duala (Republic of Cameroon). Linden-Museum, Stuttgart.

3. BAMUM. Statue of natural red-brown wood representing a standing woman with arms crossed on her stomach.
Height: 86.4 cm. Bamum (Republic of Cameroon). Museum of Primitive Art, New York.

4. BAMILEKE. Chief's throne of carved hardwood covered with dark blue and white beads. Two upright figures form the back of the seat.
Height: 190 cm. Bamileke, Baleng (Republic of Cameroon). Treasury of Bamileke Chiefdoms.

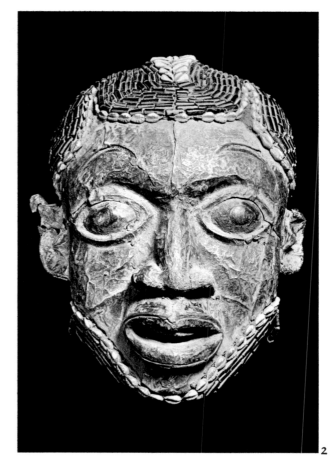

1. BAMUM. Brass-plated wooden mask with hair and beard in twisted wool.
Height: 45 cm. Bamum (Republic of Cameroon). Bafut Chiefdom.

2. BAMUM. Brass-plated wooden mask decorated with beads and cowrie-shells.
Height: 41 cm. Bamum (Republic of Cameroon). Bamenda Museum.

3. BAMUM. Mask of dark wood, very archaic in style.
Height: 31 cm. Bamum (Republic of Cameroon). André Held Collection, Ecublens.

4. BALI. Mask of dark wood with lighter patches. Stylised representation of an elephant.
Height 71,5 cm. Bali (Republic of Cameroon). British Museum, London.

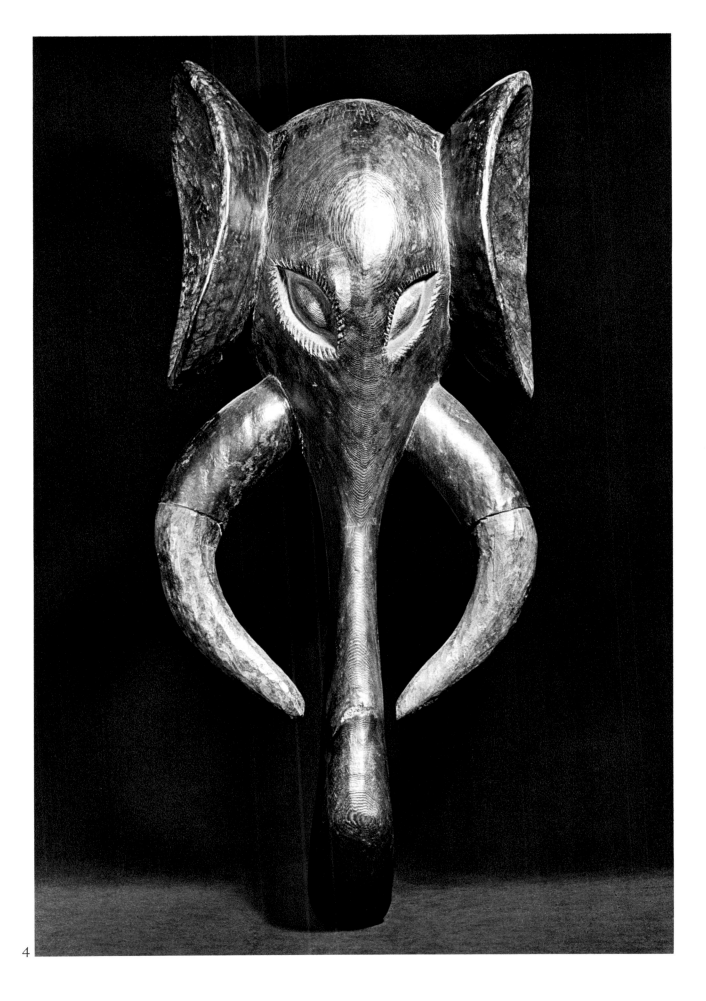

1. FANG. Statuette in wood saturated with oil, with a shiny patina. The top of the stick representing the soul of the ancestors is fixed to the *bieri* (basket containing the bones).
Height: 39 cm. Fang (Gaboon Republic). Musée des Arts Africains et Océaniens, Paris.

2. FANG. Mask of light wood white-washed with kaolin. Large face with a ghostlike appearance representing a soul.
Height: 43 cm. Fang (Gaboon Republic). Musée des Arts Africains et Océaniens, Paris.

3. FANG. Wooden statuette with 'lacquered' black patina, representing an ancestor.
Height: 59 cm. Fang (Gaboon Republic). Pierre Guerre Collection, Marseilles.

1. FANG. Statuette of blackened oiled wood. Pahuin ancestor.
Height: 64,5 cm. Fang (Gaboon Republic). Museum of Primitive Art, New York.

2. FANG. Head of light-coloured wood. The left side of the face is grainy. Brass nailheads represent the eyes.
Height: 37 cm. Fang-Pahuin (Gaboon Republic). Musée des Arts Africains et Océaniens, Paris.

3. BAKOTA. Brass- and copper-plated wooden sculpture. This funeral figure seems to wear an additional mask. Originally on a wooden shaft, now disappeared, it was planted in receptacles filled with the bones of ancestors, as among the Fang.
Height: 42 cm. Bakota (Gaboon Republic). Le Corneur Collection, Paris.

3

199

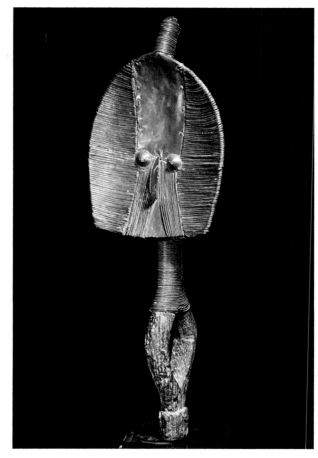

2

1. BAKOTA. Funeral figure similar to the preceding one, but completed with a wooden body whitewashed with kaolin and ending up at its base in a sort of stool. Rare example of this style.
Height: 86 cm. Bakota (Gaboon Republic). Pierre Vérité Collection, Paris.

2. OSYEBA. Wooden funeral figure covered with thin copper lamellae in parallel lines. These sculptures, called *Osyeba,* have the same ritual significance as the Bakota.
Height: 64 cm. Osyeba (Gaboon Republic). Henri Kamer Collection, Cannes.

3. BAPUNU. Mask of light wood, partly whitewashed with kaolin. Represents a soul. The hair is darkened and the mouth reddened.
Height: 35 cm. Bapunu (Gaboon Republic). Musée des Arts Africains et Océaniens, Paris.

1

1. M'BETE. Reliquary statuette of light wood white-washed with kaolin. The back, hollowed out and closed by a door, contains fragments of magic substances.
Height: 72 cm. M'Bete (Gaboon Republic). Musée des Arts Africains et Océaniens, Paris.

2. BAPUNU. Mask of light wood. The small white-washed face represents a soul. The elaborate head-gear is very dark.
Height: 31,5 cm. Bapunu (Gaboon Republic). J. Roudillon Collection, Paris.

3. KUYU. Ritual pole of natural carved wood, partly painted and topped with an owl.
Height: 113 cm. Kuyu (Gaboon Republic). Pierre Vérité Collection, Paris.

4. MITSOGO. Pillars of a sacred dwelling. These pieces of wood representing the male and female forces were fixed on either side of the door.
Height: 176 cm. Mitsogo (Gaboon Republic). Musée des Arts Africains et Océaniens, Paris.

I

3

4

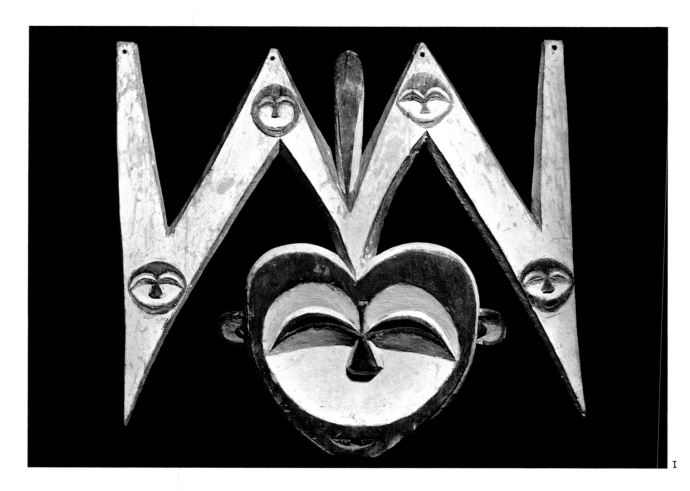

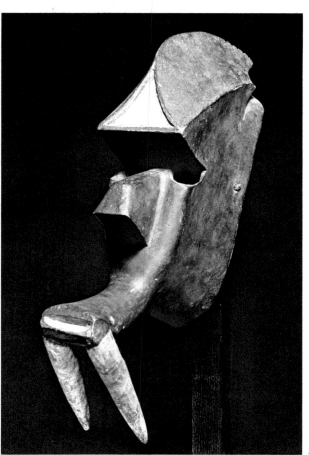

1. BAKWELE. Wooden mask painted in black and white. Flat, heart-shaped face, extended to the right and to the left by V-shaped geometrical figures. There are small masks in the same style in the angles as well as on the reverse side. The most important known work by this ethnic group.
Height: 63 cm. Bakwele (Gaboon Republic). Lafaille Natural History Museum, La Rochelle.

2. BAKWELE. Mask of darkened wood. Bold stylisation of a wild boar with yellow tusks. Frontal triangle painted with red clay.
Height: 44 cm. Bakwele (Gaboon Republic). Musée des Arts Africains et Océaniens, Paris.

3. BAKONGO. Funeral statuette carved in soft stone, representing a seated figure, with legs crossed. Ancestor figure found in a cemetery.
Height: 42.3 cm. Bakongo (Democratic Republic of the Congo). National Ethnographical Museum, Leyden.

1. BATEKE. Protective statuette of hardwood. The stomach is hollowed out and filled with magic substances kept in place by strips dyed with red "Tukula" powder. Face with parallel scarifications.
Height: 40 cm. Bateke (Republic of the Congo). Maurice Nicaud Collection, Paris.

2. BAKONGO. Female statuette of darkened wood with prominent breasts. The head is completely turned to the right – a very rare feature in African statuary art.
Height: 50,5 cm. Bakongo (Democratic Republic of the Congo). Ethnographical Museum, Antwerp.

3. LOANGO. Male mask of dark-coloured light wood emphasised by dark blue lines. A small beard of natural hair is fixed to the chin.
Height: 26 cm. Loango (Republic of the Congo). Musée des Arts Africains et Océaniens, Paris.

1

2

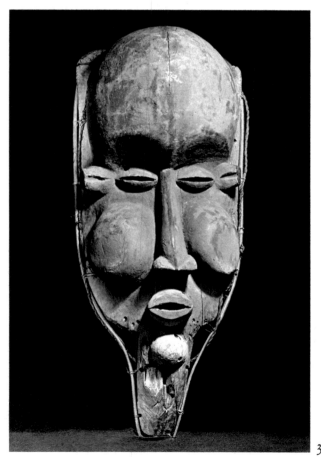

3

1. BAYAKA. Wooden mask surrounded by raffia. Used during circumcision ceremonies.
Height: 62.4 cm. Bayaka (Democratic Republic of the Congo). Royal Museum of Central Africa, Tervuren (Belgium).

2. BAYAKA. Wooden mask surrounded by raffia. Used during initiation ceremonies.
Height: 52.9 cm. Bayaka (Democratic Republic of the Congo). Royal Museum of Central Africa, Tervuren (Belgium).

3. BASUKU. Mask of reddened wood used during circumcision ceremonies.
Height: 100.6 cm. Basuku (Democratic Republic of the Congo). Royal Museum of Central Africa, Tervuren (Belgium).

4. BAPENDE. Wooden mask used during initiation ceremonies.
Height: 28.1 cm. Bapende (Democratic Republic of the Congo). Royal Museum of Central Africa, Tervuren (Belgium).

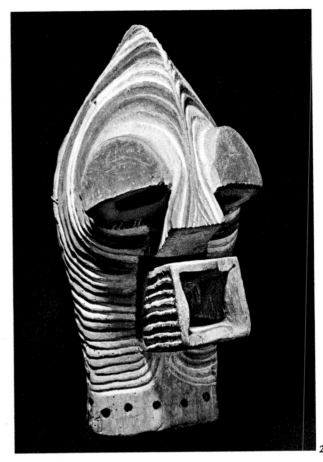

1. BENA LULUA. Wooden male statuette.
Height: 76,5 cm. Bena Lulua (Democratic Republic of
the Congo). Royal Museum of Central Africa, Tervuren
(Belgium).

2. BASONGE. *Kifwebe* mask of light wood of great
plastic boldness. All volumes converge to the eyes and
mouth, which jut forward. Curved lines, grooved and
painted, emphasize the interplay of volumes.
Height: 35,5 cm. Basonge (Democratic Republic of the
Congo). Henri Kamer Collection, Cannes.

3. BALUBA. Chief's stool, of wood, with dark brown
patina. Monoxylous. A stocky female figure supports
the seat.
Height: 47 cm. Baluba (Democratic Republic of the
Congo). Musée des Arts Africains et Océaniens, Paris.

1. BABEMBE. Large ancestor statue of heavy, dark-brown, shiny wood. Similar to the Baluba statues, its style is more stern and archaic. Undoubtedly the finest specimen known.
Height: 99.5 cm. Babembe (Republic of the Congo). René Vander Straete Collection, Brussels.

2. BALUBA. Fragment of a 'beggar' of blackened and polished wood. The arms, a portion of the legs and the cup held by the woman are missing.
Height: 27.8 cm. Baluba (Democratic Republic of the Congo). Linden-Museum, Stuttgart.

3. BAKUBA. Wooden helmet-mask. Pieces of ante-lope skin are fastened to the lower part of the face.
Height: 45.9 cm. Bakuba (Democratic Republic of the Congo). Royal Museum of Central Africa, Tervuren, (Belgium).

1

1. BAMBOLE. Slim wooden statuette. The style of the whitewashed face calls to mind certain Mitsogo and Bakwele faces.
Height: 58,5 cm. Bambole (Democratic Republic of the Congo). Joseph Van der Straete Collection, Brussels.

2. WAREGA. Ivory mask with fine dark-red patina. Remarkable for its size and quality.
Height: 22,2 cm. Warega (Democratic Republic of the Congo). Royal Museum of Central Africa, Tervuren (Belgium).

3. WAREGA. Large mask of dark wood with face of a lighter shade. The natural colour is deliberately made to reappear at certain points. One of the largest known masks in this style.
Height: 28 cm. Warega (Democratic Republic of the Congo). René Van der Straete Collection, Brussels.

1. BUKOBA. Remarkable stylisation of a bull in polished wrought iron. One of the masterpieces of iron craft.
Height: 20.5 cm. Bukoba (Tanzania, Eastern Africa). Linden-Museum, Stuttgart.

2. AZANDE. Wooden statuette representing an upright figure. A long chain with large links is suspended from the ears. Elongated torso and projecting navel.
Height: 27 cm. Azande (Democratic Republic of the Congo). Harold Rome Collection, New York.

BIBLIOGRAPHY

W. Fagg and Margaret Plass. *African Sculpture*. Dutton Vista Picturebacks. London 1964.

L. G. Pitt-Rivers. *Antique Works of Art from Benin*. London 1900.

P. Radin and J. J. Sweeney. *African Folktales and Sculptures*. New York 1952.

R. Rattray. *Religion and Art in Ashanti*. Oxford 1927.

L. Segy. *African sculpture speaks*. New York 1952.

J. J. Sweeney. *African Negro Art*. New York 1935.

L. Underwood. *Figures in wood of West Africa*. London 1947. *Masks of West Africa*. London 1948. *Bronzes of West Africa*. London 1949.

H. Baumann et D. Westermann. *Les Peuples et les Civilisations de l'Afrique*. Payot. Paris 1962.

H. Clouzot et A. Level. *L'Art nègre et l'Art océanien*. Paris 1919.

C. Einstein. *La Sculpture Africaine*. Paris 1922. (*French edition of « Afrikanische Plastik »*. Berlin 1921.)

W. Fagg et E. Elisofon. *La sculpture africaine*. F. Hazan. Paris 1960.

W. Fagg. *Les Merveilles de l'Art nigérien*. Editions du Chêne. Paris 1963.

L. Frobenius. *Histoire de la Civilisation Africaine*. Gallimard. Paris 1936.

J. Girard. *Dynamique de la Société Ouobé. Loi des Masques et Coutumes*. Institute of Black Africa.

R. Goldwater. *Bambara Sculpture of the Western Sudan*. New York 1960.

M. Griaule. *Masques Dogons*. Paris 1963.

M. Griaule. *Arts de l'Afrique Noire*. Editions du Chêne. Paris 1947.

G. Hardy. *L'Art Nègre. L'Art animiste des noirs d'Afrique*. Paris 1927.

C. Kjersmeier. *Centres de styles de la sculpture africaine*. Paris - Copenhagen 1935-38 (4 volumes).

H. Lachavery. *Statuaire de l'Afrique Noire*. Neuchâtel 1954.

J. Laude. *Les Arts de l'Afrique noire*. Le Livre de Poche. Paris 1966.

J.-P. Lebeuf et A. Masson-Detourbet. *La Civilisation du Tchad*. Paris 1953.

R. Lecocq. *Les Bamiléké, une civilisation africaine*. Paris 1953.

M. Leiris. *Les Nègres et les Arts sculpturaux*. Paris. Unesco 1954.

M. Leiris et J. Delange. *Afrique Noire — La Création Plastique*. Gallimard. Paris 1967.

H. Lem. *Sculptures Soudanaises*. Paris 1948.

E. Leuzinger. *Afrique. L'art des peuples noirs*. Albin Michel. Paris 1962.

A. Maesen. *« Umbangu » — Art du Congo au Musée de Tervuren*. Editions Cultura. Brussels 1960.

J. Maquet. *Afrique — Les Civilisations noires*. Horizons de France. Paris 1962.

Le Musée Vivant. Numéro spécial sur l'Afrique. Paris, November 1948.

F. Olbrechts. *Plastiek van Kongo*. Brussels 1947.

M. Palau-Marti. *Le Roi-Dieu au Bénin*. Berger-Levrault. Paris 1964.

D. Paulme. *Les sculptures de l'Afrique Noire*. Presses Universitaires de France. Paris 1956.

D. Paulme. *L'Art sculptural Nègre* (2 volumes). Paris 1962.

D.-P. de Pedrals. *Archéologie de l'Afrique Noire*. Payot. Paris 1950.

Présence Africaine. L'Art Nègre, 10 et 11. Paris 1951.

R. Rasmussen. *Art Nègre*. Paris 1951.

C. Roy. *Les Arts sauvages*. Delpire. Paris 1957.

A. Terrisse. *L'Afrique de l'Ouest, berceau de l'Art Nègre*. Introduction by L. S. Senghor. Nathan 1965.

D. Zahan. *Sociétés d'initiation Bambara*. Paris 1960.

217

GLOSSARY

Ade.   Royal hat in the shape of a tiara, decorated and surrounded by a fringe of beads concealing the face.

Afin.   Royal palace.

Aggris, Aggreys or *Aigris.*   Beads cut from blue stone, reserved for kings.

Akan.   Collective term used to designate the southern ethnic groups of the former Gold Coast, now Ghana. Extends to the Ivory Coast and includes the Ebrie and other people of the lagoon areas.

Bakota-Hongwe.   Bakota sub-tribe, which has produced highly architectural helmet-masks with a single face.

Bantu.   Word which means 'men' and which designates several south and west African tribes with a common philosophy and language.

Bobo-Fing.   The Bobo are divided into three distinct groups:
— Bobo-Fing : black Bobo.
— Bobo-Gbe : white Bobo.
— Bobo-Ule : red Bobo.

Chi wara.   Means: 'The features of labour and of the earth' (see Dominique Zahan). In a wider sense, defines the Bambara helmet crests representing the male and female antelope.

Cowrie.   Shells found mainly in the Indian Ocean; for a long time they were used as money in Africa; they are also used in decorative and magical art objects. In Negro sculpture, the eye is frequently derived from the shape of the cowrie, if it is not itself a cowrie.

Dagacin.   Name of the Jebba chief in northern Nigeria.

Egbora.   Temple. The figure 201 equals 200 plus one, this figure evoking 'all human possibilities'.

Ekiti.   Nigerian ethnic group which has produced some remarkable wrought-iron objects. Most of them represent groups of birds, while others are symbols deriving from the curve of animals horns.

Emese.   Servant attached to the king.

Emewa.   Chief of the exterior who commands a part of the city.

Fa.   Divination process among the Yoruba, which utilises a wooden tray containing vegetable powder. The wizard, having transferred Kola nuts from his right hand to his left hand, traces signs according to the figure obtained. He then interprets this figure to answer the question which has been asked.

Gelede.   Yoruba mask of the keitu society (Dahomey), surmounted by a great variety of plastic decorations, either ritual or symbolic and anecdotal.

Gla or *Tehegla.*   Mask representing male beauty.

Guli.   Mask of a buffalo, used in a nocturnal dance. It is accompanied by a horn-player. Divine in essence, it chases away bad luck, dispels demons, and cripples the power of sorcerers.

218

Holo.   See Nzambi-Holo.

Kanaga.   Famous Dogon mask in the shape of the Cross of Lorraine, used during funeral rituals.

Kebe-Kebe.   Wooden head ending up in a handle, used by the Kuyu during dances.

Kifwebe.   Powerful Basonge mask engraved with painted parallel lines. Has exercised great influence on modern art.

Kore.   Means: 'man's destiny' among the Bambara.

Kple.   Round and horned Baule mask, consisting of a flat disc in light wood, only the eyes and lips being in slight relief.

Kuduo.   Bronze or brass receptacle designed to contain gold dust. It was buried in the tombs of important chiefs.

Lajodogun.   Hall of the royal palace, dedicated to Ogun, god of the ironsmiths.

Manilla.   Bronze piece in the shape of a bracelet, of Portuguese origin. Introduced in West Africa about the sixteenth century, it was used as money until recently. The metal of the Benin bronzes and famous plaques is the product of melting down manillae.

Mbuya.   Best-known Bapende mask used in rituals following the circumcision of young men.

Monomotapa.   Ancient kingdom in South-East Africa, a gold mine area.

N'Domo.   Bambara initiation society practising progressive revelation for non-circumcised children (see D. Zahan).

Nilotic.   Races of the Upper Nile with negroid features but light skin. Related to Ethiopia, they have peopled a part of Nubia.

Nzambi-Holo.   Openwork sculpture reproducing a figure with spread-out arms. Deriving from Christian representations of Christ introduced in the Congo and in Angola by missionaries in the sixteenth century, it eventually resumed an animistic significance. It is an example of African syncretism, the word Nzambi meaning God.

Occrah.   Royal personage among the Ashanti.

Oranmiyan.   Sovereign considered to be the founder of the royal dynasty.

Ox-pecker.   White bird of the wader family which settles on the back of oxen and relieves them of vermin. It is featured on Baule and Senufo doors.

Tapa.   A sort of felted cloth made from tree-bark which is soaked, and then expanded and made supple with the hammer.

Tellem.   Predecessors of the Dogon. They have produced statuettes with arms usually raised in imploration of rain. They are covered with a grey, brown or reddish crust made up of a mixture of birdseeds, blood and earth. The oldest date from the thirteenth or fourteenth century.

Tukula or *N'Gula.*   Red wood dust from the *pterocarpus* or camwood tree. Used as medicine, and, when mixed with palm oil, as cosmetic ointment. The Bakuba kept this powder in beautiful boxes decorated with geometrical motifs.

Yaure.   Small ethnic group who live between the Baule and the Guro. Some details of their masks are derived from these two neighbours, and their style is a sort of synthesis of both neighbouring styles.

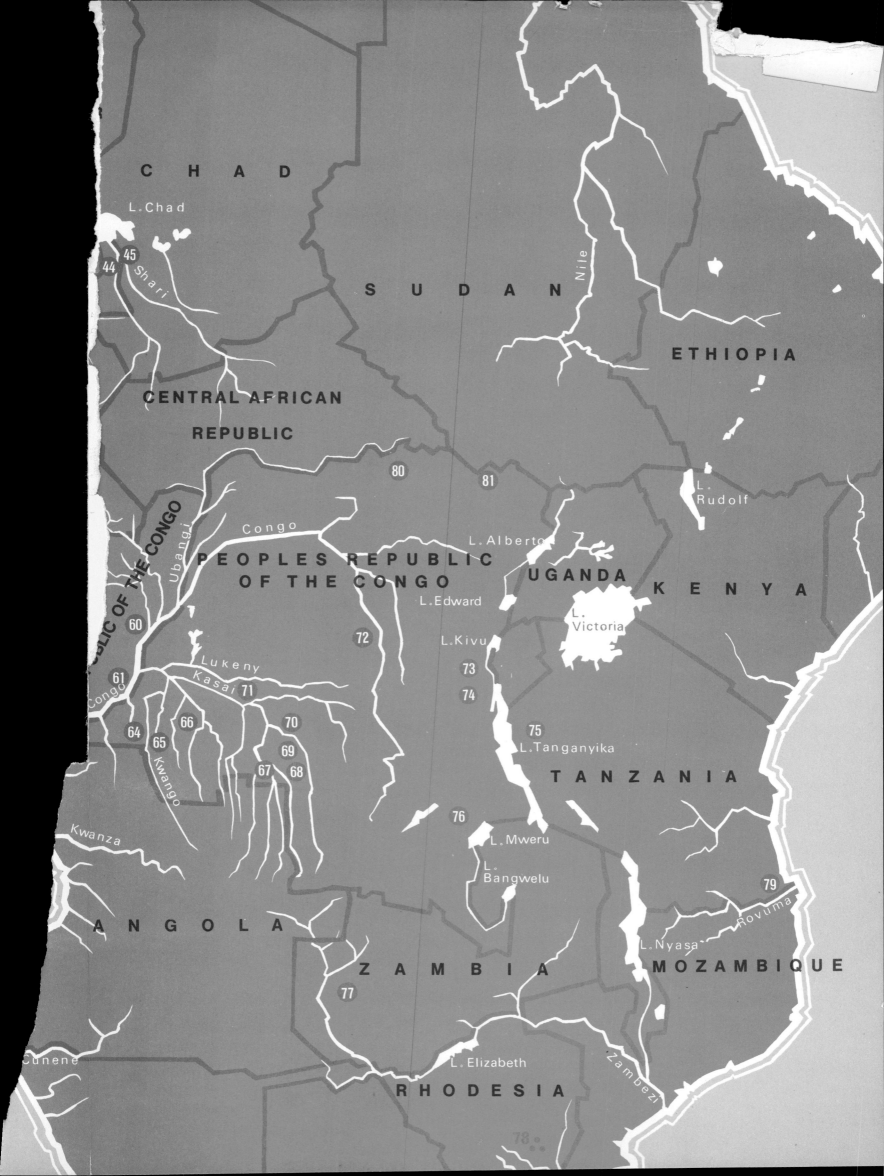

MAURETANIA

Senegal

SENEGAL

GAMBIA

MALI

NIGE

PORT.
GUINEA

GUINEA

SIERRA
LEONE

LIBERIA

IVORY
COAST

VOLTA

GHANA

TOGO

DAHOMEY

NIGERIA

Niger

Benue

Volta

Niger

CAMEROON

Sanaga

SPANISH
GUINEA

GABOON

Ogowé

REP.

Afade 44	Bayaka 64	Kuyu 60
Afo 38	Bena Lulua 69	Loango 62
Agni 16	Benin 34	Lobi 22
Akan 21	Bidjogo 1	Lower Niger 35
Ashanti 20	Bobo 23	Makonde 79
Attie 15	Bukoba 75	Mama 43
Azande 80	Dan 13	Mangbetu 81
Babembe 74	Dogon 25	Marka 26
Baga 2	Duala 53	M'Bete 57
Bajokwe 67	Ekoi 50	Mende 4
Bakongo 63	Ewe 29	Mitsogo 58
Bakota 56	Fang 54	Mossi 28
Bakuba 70	Fon 30	N'Dengese 71
Bakwele 55	Guro 19	N'Gere 11
Bali 47	Ibibio 51	Nok 42
Baluba 76	Ibo 37	Nupe 41
Bambara 24	Ife 33	Oron 52
Bambole 72	Ijo 36	Sao 45
Bamileke 49	Jebba 40	Senufo 9
Bamum 48	Keitu 31	Sherbro 3
Bapende 66	Kissi 5	Tada 39
Bapunu 59	Kono 8	Toma 6
Barotse 77	Kotoko 46	Warega 73
Basonge 68	Kran 12	Wobe 10
Basuku 65	Krinjabo 14	Yaure 18
Bateke 61	Kru 7	Yoruba 32
Baule 17	Kurumba 27	Zimbabwe 78